D1518421

RUN-OUT GROOVE:

Inside Capitol's 1980s Hits & Stiffs

The Morrell Archives Volume 4

Dave Morrell

Credits:
Edited by Brenda Hanson
Cover Design by Jack Snyder
Special thanks to Judi Kerr for her continued support and love.
Copyright © 2020 Dave Morrell All rights reserved.
ISBN: 9798623742681
Typeset by Amnet Systems.

Table of Contents

Preface

As I was completing "45 RPM (Recollections Per Minute): The Morrell Archives Volume 3," I happened to watch "La Ronde," the 1950 film directed by Max Ophüls and based on Arthur Schnitzler's play of the same name. The master of ceremonies asks, "And me? What part do I play in the story…The author? An accomplice? A passerby? I am you. That is, any one of you. I am the personification of your desire to know everything."

He goes on to tell us, "I see all sides…because I see in the round."

With this book, I hope to show you sides you haven't seen of an industry that romances and seduces you into giving up your soul. It twists and whirls your senses with overwhelmingly fantabulous music.

It's always New Year's Eve.

We worked around the clock, eight days a week and only the strong survived. The others were blown to smithereens.

Just where are we?

Backstage at Max's Kansas City?

Dave Morrell

In the Ballroom of the Waldorf-Astoria?
On air at WNEW-FM?
We are on a street.
We are in New York City.
It's 1980.

From an office on 56th Street, we gain a panoramic view of the music industry, supersizing the excesses of the era. Chasing stiffs as if they were hits, paying shady indie promotion figures big spiffs (bonuses) and nearly bungling mega records like Duran Duran's "Hungry Like The Wolf" and Crowded House's "Don't Dream It's Over."

The phone rings... It has been weaponized by the rumpdogs. They are spinning, spinning, spinning out of control in a circular building located almost 3,000 miles away – the Capitol Records Tower.

One boss has a cattle prod in his office. Another favors sledgehammers.

They have some select words for the promotion staff, charged with getting radio stations to play the label's singles.

"Bring in the kneepads, bring in a baseball bat! We need stations on this record."

"Bob Seger's 'Like A Rock' is a goddamn embarrassment! We gotta go top 10!!"

"Give away all the Beatles records you need to get the job done!"

"For fuck's sake, what the hell is going on out there!"

"Don't tell me you got dinner plans or some shit! Get on the road!"

"Go sell your soul to the Devil! I don't care. We have to have 10 adds!"

"It's countdown time to losing your jobs!"

The staff takes the beatdown and reaches for a bump up. It's the 80's – decades before bigwigs have to worry about the fallout of a toxic work culture. My characters turn…and turn…and turn.

Chapter 1

Hanging Up the Hit 45s

The district manager, seated across the desk from me at Capitol Records' Manhattan office, looked me in the eye and asked, "Do you smoke pot?"

I froze. Should I lie?

I leaned forward and whispered, "Yes."

"Good!" he yelled. "You're in! Can you get to Hollywood tomorrow? I want you to meet your new boss."

In eight years, I'd gone from being Assistant Stock Boy in the eight-track tape department at the Warner/Elektra/Atlantic warehouse distribution center in New Jersey to working 45s at top 40 radio for Warner Bros. and RCA Records. Now Capitol Records – the label that introduced the Beatles to America – wanted me to work their albums at rock radio. I was 26 years old.

It was time for me to hang up the old 45.

Back in the Old West, a 45 could stop you in your tracks. In 1964 "She Loves You" stopped me and the rest of the world in our tracks!

I had been working the 45 since I arrived on the promotion scene in 1972. I'd had a hand in breaking hits like "Midnight at the Oasis" by Maria Muldaur, "Tin Man" by America and "Sundown" by Gordon Lightfoot.

Working top 40 was a bitch. It was hard. I had to deal with New York City, where stations paid massive amounts of money for research. There was no getting around it. If you weren't in the top 30 with sales in the market, it would be tough to get WABC to look at your record. Sure, there were a few flukes like "MacArthur Park," which you knew in one listen was a hit. "American Pie" was like that and, come to think of it, both songs were longer than most 45s.

WABC always wanted records that were under three minutes. One time we brought "Dueling Banjos" up there, but it was a little over 3 minutes. Instead of editing, we just changed the time on the record. Once the PD caught on, he told us he wasn't going to play it if we didn't cut it. We went back to the studio but instead of editing, we just speeded it up! It worked!! They never caught on until we brought the original guys up to the station to play the song in the PD's office. As they were dueling it out, the PD was clapping his hands and stamping his feet, yelling "FASTER!!!"

When I worked the 45, I had to spend a tremendous amount of energy hyping the stores with tickets and t-shirts to get them to tell the radio station MY

SINGLES WERE SELLING! I hated that end of the business.

At WABC I learned that a few of the jocks were in the music meetings, so I tried to find out who they were. I figured the guy that got off the air at 10 a.m. was probably asked to attend, but the guy on the air wouldn't be in the meeting. With that thought process, I'd call the morning guy on the request line and ask for a song I knew they weren't playing. He'd ask me if I heard it on the station and I'd tell him I hear it everywhere! I figured if my song was in the music meeting, he'd pipe up and say he was getting requests!

While I was driving myself crazy coming up with schemes to get songs added at top 40, the album guy at Warner was hosting DJs at the office, giving away free albums and smoking pot all day! Of course, he needed to have great knowledge of the personal tastes of all the DJs that are on the air – so he was constantly taking them out to breakfast, lunch or dinner. It seemed like a pretty sweet gig.

Now I would be the album guy at Capitol, required only to work rock albums to rock stations and deal only with rock programmers. One Capitol boss would call the few of us that worked rock stations "wine and cheese party planners." After years of working top 40, it sure wasn't offensive to me. I looked forward to it!

Chapter 2

Keys to Rock

I was handed the keys to Capitol's rock 'n' roll albums. No more disco records. No more R&B, no more country and no more top 40!

From now on, it was just listening to rock 'n' roll!

To cut to the chase, on rock albums, it was usually the first song on the first side that got all the traction. This prime spot is where the artist and the label would put their focus track. It made it easier for the DJs to find.

The FM stations didn't even have playlists. They played records in either a heavy, medium or light rotation and reported that to the trades.

From now on, instead of asking record stores to report my songs to the radio stations, I would just have to try and make sure the DJ would front and back announce the song and artist they were playing.

One of the hot ideas Capitol's Ray Tusken, VP of Promotion, came up with was elevating the listeners' experience. Ray would insist on a 12" of the focus song, then a hot new-mix, then he got us to resend the album using a higher-grade vinyl that made the sound JUMP! After a few weeks of airplay, Ray would always produce a hotter sound for the airwaves.

Ray was based in Hollywood, but I would work out of Capitol's office on 56th Street in Manhattan. As Associate National AOR Promotion Director, I'd have local promotion managers in NYC, Boston, Hartford, Philadelphia, Washington DC, Nashville, Atlanta, Miami, Cincinnati, Cleveland and Detroit reporting to me. My job was to help them deliver their rock stations. That meant I had to not only call my staff, but also their key rock programmers.

Sometimes I had better relationships with the radio program director than I did with the local Capitol representative.

Chapter 3

In the Beginning

By the time I got to Capitol Records, a man named Al Coury had left the building. He had been the head of promotion and influenced many people who followed him. Al was followed by Bruce Wendell, who was now leading the Capitol promotion team.

Bruce had this to say about his mentor.

"Al stepped on a lot of toes! He pushed aside the lame and the slow. He put sledgehammers on our desks to remind us to HAMMER!!! HAMMER!!!"

Al was loud. He was a screamer. If you weren't on the receiving end, it would all seem cruel and over the top.

Bruce was just like that.

After I was hired, I flew to Los Angeles and went to the iconic Capitol Tower in Hollywood – the round one that looks like a stack of 45s on a big spindle – to meet Bruce and the rest of the folks. I spent less than a minute with him. He wished me good luck!

Everyone I met told me Bruce was Mr. Hollywood. He was successful, good looking, lived in Beverly Hills, had a house in Palm Springs, drove a Rolls Royce and dated some of the hottest Hollywood starlets.

Although Mr. Hollywood was my boss, I was part of the rock department that fell under Ray Tusken's direction, so I wouldn't have much contact with Bruce.

Mr. Hollywood would lead the weekly conference calls and, like his predecessor, he could also step on toes, push aside the lame and slow and HAMMER HAMMER!!!

Chapter 4

Throwing Punches And Cranking
Up The Beatles "Rarities"

After I returned to the chilly East Coast, the mailman brought my new Capitol Records employee ID card. It felt great.

Capitol was coming off 1979 with a monster one-hit wonder by the Knack called "My Sharona." The band went from a park bench to Park Avenue with the sales of that record. By the time I arrived, they released their follow-up album "But The Little Girls Understand," and we were working the track "Hold On Tight and Don't Let Go" to rock radio. Things had changed and it was hard to come up with anything from the new record that was sticking. The band failed to connect at top 40 with "Baby Talks Dirty," and "Can't Put A Price On Love" – neither of which charted. In 1981 they came back with "Round Trip," but it didn't catch on either.

I began attending all the Capitol performances in New York City. McGuinn – Hillman minus Gene Clark, whose health was ailing, came to play the Bottom Line. Turns out, Chris Hillman's wife was sitting earshot from the New York A&R man for Capitol. Apparently, he had some unkind words about the show he was witnessing. Once the show was over, we all headed backstage but didn't get far. Chris wound up and punched the A&R rep in the head. He went right down to the floor. We saw the action and headed straight for the exit. The A&R guy didn't last much longer at Capitol.

My mind was only half on the action since I was carrying an advance cassette of the new Beatles "Rarities" album and I wanted to be home listening to it on my stereo. A guy at the Capitol Tower in Los Angeles put it together, but it would have to wait.

It was 10 p.m. and I still had to hop uptown to see Capitol artist Eve Moon play at Traxx. It was on 72nd Street, down the block from where John Lennon was living. Eve was Willy DeVille's backup singer and sang on the classic album "Le Chat Bleu," which was a top 10 favorite amongst all the critics that year. Unfortunately, Capitol didn't think much of the album and released it only in Europe.

I finally got home around 2 a.m. and called the guy at Capitol on the West Coast to go over the Beatles "Rarities" album. I knew it was going to be special if this guy's fingerprints were on it. Turns out, he had both hands on it!

I called and he picked right up. He was a night owl too!

He said, "It's a long story. In 1979 they were ready to issue the UK version of the album here in America. In fact, store copies without covers actually do exist! But I was able to stop Capitol from releasing the NON-"Rarities" UK LP here. I talked them into the USA idea, complete with the Butcher uncropped photo from "Yesterday and Today" for the front cover, but they decided to use it inside the gatefold."

It was time to hang up and throw up the volume! I didn't care what time I got to sleep.

The cassette contained 15 tracks of the Beatles with alternative mixes. Not a ground breaker, but interesting. It wasn't coming out yet, but with this advance cassette I could start playing it for all the FM programmers.

I was so excited! It was my first chance to actually work a Beatles album!

I kept my Beatles fever as low as possible when I joined Capitol. I didn't want to overwhelm any-one with my obvious enthusiasm. I always loved the Beatles and had a gathered together quite a collec-tion. I even thought if I ever met a Beatle, they would get a kick out some of the oddball memorabilia that came out. Perhaps they were so busy they didn't get to see some of the nonsense. Believe it or not, I had that very experience with John Lennon. And YES – he did get a great big kick out of it! I showed him album covers he was unaware of like "The Savage Young Beatles" which showed the boys in their full leather gear. He loved that one!

It was all such great fun and now, here I was, a Beatles fan working a Beatles album. It was something I can even call "OFFICIAL."

Well the "Rarities" turned out to be what they call a catalog item meaning they weren't going to spend money marketing it or promoting it. It would be a low-key event.

One thing it did do was to bring me closer to the programmers who loved the Beatles. As our paths would cross my collection would grow and grow and grow. The best thing of all? The cool people in radio loved to talk about the Beatles as much as I did and that made my job a whole lot easier.

Chapter 5

Bootlegville

Keith was the guy in Greenwich Village that ran the roost. He was super organized and had worked at a half a dozen downtown record shops before owning one himself. He made his headquarters on the second floor of a building directly across the street from Electric Lady Studios. We're talking about 8th Street between McDougal (where Dylan once lived) and Sixth Avenue, which is also called the Avenue of the Americas. It was a sweet spot.

Keith's shop was the place everyone wanted to visit. He was getting material from the *Rolling Stone* writers, *The New York Times* writers and even stuff from managers and artists. Keith had something for everyone that walked in the door. Most of the time it was illegal, but nobody minded. The walls were covered with rare Beatles, Stones and Dylan records. There were rare 50's albums, fan magazines, memorabilia and the most sought-after bootleg recordings. Stuff nobody else had.

Keith said it all came tumbling down from Stan. Stan was from Sweden and had been putting out vinyl bootleg albums for years. He was in a league of his own. The quality of sound he got from master tapes was extraordinary and his liner notes, done by a well know Beatle collector under a synonym to remain anonymous, were above most Beatle collectors' knowledge. The final artwork on his discs was better than the graphics Capitol Records was putting out. It got so crazy for him that when George Harrison's lawyer sent a letter of cease and desist, Stan used the letter for the cover of his next bootleg George Harrison release.

Stan would ship over compact discs that were mislabeled to look like Shakespearian speeches or Beethoven classical music. Nobody in customs would see anything unusual. Keith would be in charge of receiving the packages and keeping them under lock and key until Stan arrived. His brother was a pilot and Stan would fly free and actually get to sit in the cockpit. Stan didn't take baggage since he wasn't staying long in NY.

Keith would organize the Village shop owners and they'd meet at Café' Reggio on MacDougal Street. This great joint has the original espresso machine, made in 1902, that the owner bought when he opened the café back in 1927. They even filmed *The Godfather Part ll* here which made sense to Keith since this whole business was cloak and dagger.

They'd grab a table and sit in a circle. Stan would arrive carrying a box that was full of the CD inserts. This was the artwork that would go with the discs Keith had stashed back at his shop. It was eye-opening to see what Stan had to offer. On this occasion, Stan delivered an incredible cache of rare Beatle tapes.

Stan had secured an EMI recording session of the Beatles from June and September of 1962, plus another long master tape from March and September of 1963. Everyone was stunned.

The group of store owners had $5,000 in cash and each guy put the money in a brown paper bag. Stan collected all the bags and put the cash into a money belt. Then he put the belt around his waist and put his shirt over it to hide it all.

Stan passed around the inserts. He said he'd be back soon with more wonderous and mind-blowing material. And with that said, he laid a cassette tape on Keith with some goodies, he hugged everyone and said his goodbyes. He never spent the night.

These discs would come to market and, in some cases, command a $35 price tag. Uncle Sam wasn't counting these discs. The market was in a frenzy and Keith was the Godfather.

Once someone broke into the car of Michael Lang, one of the guys that had put on the Woodstock festival. The thief found a suitcase full of cassettes, so he took them to Keith's place. Michael Lang had been managing Joe Cocker and the tapes were full of music Joe was working on. Keith did the right thing. He bought them and contacted Michael to see that he got his personal belongings back.

There was a side of Keith only a few knew about. It was Keith's ability to score some very high-grade pharmaceutical cocaine. Not to mention the very best grass anyone was smoking. He had Collie weed from Jamaica, Panama Red from Mexico, Thai Sticks from Vietnam and Mowie Wowie from Hawaii.

I'd go down to Keith's a few times a week to hang out and catch up on the underground scene. Keith would always let me borrow anything just so I could hear cool stuff. I'd bring all the artists I worked with down to his shop after hours. Duran Duran would shop there. So would the guys from Iron Maiden, especially bass player Steve Harris. Steve was so cool he'd personally call the store and put all the employees on the list for tickets and backstage passes for any upcoming Iron Maiden shows.

Chapter 6

Jeff Beck Electric Lady Listening Session

It's 4 a.m. Greenwich Village time and no one wants to call it quits for the night. We're all in the back of Keith's shop, talking about nothing with a head full of drugs when all of a sudden the phone rings. We all figure our man was getting an international call from overseas asking about some rare Beatles memorabilia, but it's actually Sally who works across the street. It's late and she's heading home but she saw the light on and thought she'd ask what was going on. My friend invites her to stop in. Turns out she works at Electric Lady Studios, the former nightclub that Jimi Hendrix had converted into a recording studio. As she got settled, she told us she had been working late keeping the studio open for Jeff Beck. We were all fans of Jeff. You could tell she had just heard some incredibly innovative music all evening.

I'm not sure if a half hour passed or a half a gram of coke passed, but she jolted us out of our stupor when she said, "Wanna go back to the studio and hear the tapes?"

"WHA????"

She said, "Yeah, I got the keys and the tape is on the machine. All I have to do is push the start button. It's easy, let's go!"

We all marched over and made our way into what once was the Jimi Hendrix studio. We were way out of our league.

We listened while lying on the floor, staring at the ceiling. It was incredible. Just twenty minutes earlier, I had been thumbing through old used albums at a place with a bathroom that was straight out of CBGB's basement.

Hearing Jeff in Jimi's living room at top volume was sensational. Jeff was jamming!

Chapter 7

CBGB

In 1970, I was prowling the Lower East Side during the day and by night I was discovering new live music at the Fillmore East. Here it was, 10 years later, and I'm still pulling all-nighters down in the Bowery, only now I'm at CBGB's.

Hilly Kristal owned and ran the joint. He was an incredible guy who had a history of owning clubs in the Village. He was a big man with a grizzly beard. His voice was deep, but I never heard him yell or raise his voice at anyone. He also managed and produced a few bands. We became friends when Capitol signed his band called the Shirts. The band was fronted by Annie Golden, who went on to star in the motion picture version of *Hair*.

Hilly had quite an ear for music. One night around 2 a.m. we were both bullshitting, and he mentioned a few new bands he had high hopes for. He had a tall cold beer in one hand and a pile of cassettes in the other.

"Dave, ya gotta hear these! I got the 'Screamin' Sneakers, The Same, Blue Fire, The Y-Pants and a hot group I want you to hear right now. They're about to take the stage."

"What's it sound like?" I asked him.

"The kid sounds like a moose in heat!!!" he shouted in my ear.

"Whoa! Sounds dangerous!!!" I yelled back.

"The band is called the Pet Clams!! They got a record called 'Big Fat Pet Clams From Outer Space!' I produced it!" he was proud to say.

I yelled to the bartender to bring me a double. It was going to be a long night.

Chapter 8

Graham Nash

It was a beautiful April spring day in New York City. In fact, it was the first day of the year you could go outside without a coat. Graham Nash, who was in town to promote his new album, was heading up to WNEW FM. Usually just the promo man and maybe a photographer make the trip to the station, but everyone at Capitol loved Graham so we all went to the station. The press people, the sales guys and even the jocks that weren't on the air came to the station to meet Graham. It was 1980, four months after the No Nukes concerts at Madison Square Garden which ended up as a three-record set.

The great (now late) disc jockey Pete Fornatale did the mid-day interview and he kicked it off by playing the title track from Graham's latest album, "Earth & Sky." Good vibrations were all around Graham.

The interview went great and 45 minutes later Pete was ready to wrap it up.

Pete – "Let's remind the people once again, you are in town for a major showcase appearance Saturday evening, April 26th, at the Palladium Theater. Show begins at 8pm. Leah Kunkel opens the show. I wanted to conclude by asking you a question I think has relevance to what you're doing these days. You have had major success now in the 60's, your days with the Hollies and then followed that with even more amazing success stories in the 70's, Crosby, Stills, Nash and Young. What is Graham Nash up to in the 80's? What do you look to accomplish with your career in this decade?"

Graham – "I've always approached it from the point of view that I'm just thankful and grateful to get up every morning and take that first breath. As long as I can keep doing that, I will keep on creating. Hopefully, I will keep on expanding as a person. I will keep on trying to be a better person as I can be and as considerate as I can be. I wanna slip through this life like an arrow. I just wanna zip right through it to whatever's coming next."

Pete – "Now you have seen music in all its changes over the course of the two past decades and it certainly is in a state of change right now. What about your place in that? Do you think there's a tendency for material like you have on the 'Earth & Sky' album to be overlooked in this atmosphere? Are you concerned about that?"

Graham – "It's possible, it's possible there are people out there that don't wanna listen to this stuff, but that's not my concern. My concern is only for my own selfish psychiatric reasons. I talk to myself internally a great deal. I work out a lot of my problems in my music and I never paid a psychiatric bill yet and I have no intentions of doing so. So, as long as I can keep getting my feelings out and have a vehicle for them, I will remain sane."

Pete- "Continued success! Thanks for coming over."

We all headed out to lunch and afterwards we wished Graham the best of luck on his new release.

A few days later Graham was down in Philadelphia about to make the rounds when all of a sudden, the local promotion guy called in sick and I had to race down to cover for him on short notice.

Of course, being a collector of Beatles stuff, I wanted to talk to Graham about the 60's. I was a big Hollies fan and hoped we'd get a chance to step back, but at this point Graham was living in the moment.

I parked the car and told the guys the station was right down the block. As we began to walk, a couple of bums were starting a fight and it was spilling on to the street. Graham asked me if we could go around the block to avoid the conflict.

As we walked around beautiful Rittenhouse Square where the station was located, Graham noticed a record shop. To my delight, he asked me if we had time to go in. I said yes and followed him into the store.

Graham walked right up to the man behind the counter and looked him straight in the eye and asked, "Have you got any bootlegs on Joni Mitchell?"

I looked at the clerk who clearly didn't recognize Graham Nash.

The guy said, "No, but I got a few on the Grateful Dead! Wanna have a look?"

"I'll pass," said Graham and then added, "Got any Crosby, Stills, Nash and Young bootlegs?"

"Nope," said the salesman.

So off we went.

It did light a bulb on my head! Graham is into bootlegs!

After the radio interview, we climbed back into my car and headed back to the hotel where Graham was staying.

Graham was in a good mood and was smiling when I said to him, "I collect Beatles bootlegs and rare tapes. I've got a good one for you if you're interested. It's the Beatles demo tape made in January of 1962."

He nodded yes and I put it on.

He was totally enthralled and focused on the primitive sound and then he just lost his cool!

The tape began to play Leiber and Stroller's classic "Searchin,'" performed by the Beatles and sung by Paul McCartney.

Graham started waving his hands and yelling at me to TURN IT UP!

He was flipping out. He yelled, "Beep the horn! Flash the lights!"

Then he delightfully told the tale.

He said it was one of the first things the Hollies did and he sang on it! He couldn't believe he was hearing the Beatles singing it here in the car in 1980!

The moment really broke the ice for us.

He said he had to have it! I told him he could have this tape!

He flipped. He then told me how he'd written "Marrakesh Express" and tried to record it for the Hollies. He said it didn't work out so he left and formed Crosby, Stills and Nash. He took the song to them and it became their first single. Graham said he had a copy of the Hollies version and that he'd be happy to make a copy for me.

Once we split up and I headed home, I called all my collector friends to pull together a Hollies reel of TV appearances over the years on shows like "Shindig," "Hullaballoo," "The Ed Sullivan Show" and many more.

One night Graham was doing a solo show up in Paramus, New Jersey and he told me to bring the gang to his hotel room so we could watch the old shows. We set up a 16 mm machine in his room and began to blow Graham's mind. Just as clips began, he'd tell us what clothes he'd be wearing and where he got them. "Dear Eloise" was one of his favorites, plus we had a color print of the performance, which really made his clothes stand out.

When the afternoon was over, Graham invited everyone to his show. Standing by the side of the stage, I saw Graham deliver one of the best solo shows I've ever seen. Graham is a passionate story-teller and it feels like he's speaking directly to you.

We stayed in touch until Graham left the label. His album didn't do well. "Barrel of Pain" was the song we went with to the FM stations. It was an important message, but never made it to heavy rotation. We tried another cut, but the record just didn't connect.

Chapter 9

Carole King 1980

I came back from lunch and there was a message for me that said Carole King called. I gulped and asked the girl who took the message what this was about. She said she didn't know. I asked her if she knew if this was the real Carole King, the one who did the "Tapestry" album. She said she didn't know. I took a long breath and called the number. A woman answered and said, "Yes, can I help you?" I said, "This is Dave Morrell," and before I could finish, she yelled into the phone, "My promotion man Dave!" I asked if this was Carole and she said, "Yes, it's Carole King and I want to say hello and let you know I am available for interviews."

I was blown away. It was really rare to get a call from an artist directly. I knew I would walk over hot coals for her new album. It was an album called "Pearls – Songs of Goffin and King."

"Dave, can I have your full support?" she asked.

I looked down on my list of airplay priorities carefully before I answered. I saw the Elektrics, the Shirts, and Sweet and replied. "Yes, you can expect 100% from me."

"One Fine Day" became a Top 15 track and we followed it with "Oh No Not My Baby."

Nothing happened for the Shirts, the Elektrics or the Sweet record, but they were fun to work with.

Stephen from Sweet was hell bent on horror books and movies at the moment, so when I had to take him out to Long Island to promote his new band's record, he demanded we head over to the Amityville Horror home. To me it looked like any other house on any other block, but when we got out of the car Stephen wouldn't go near it. We asked him if he wanted his photo taken with him standing by the house, but he wouldn't do it. He really thought it was haunted.

On the other hand, Annie from the Shirts wasn't sure what was going on. She seemed over her head when it came to doing interviews. She wasn't a real punk. The band had tried many different attempts at a sound, and I'm not sure punk was the right way to go. Missing Persons from Los Angeles was making a splash with a similar sound and soon the Shirts drowned.

The Elektrics were a solid power pop band that called themselves the 80's before changing it up. We did everything we could to move the needle and help them. We did live radio broadcasts with them at multiple radio stations, we did the silly Uncle Floyd TV cult show that hipsters were following and they had good bookings like the Bottom Line club in NYC. The album was done at the Power Station recording studio with Bon Jovi's brother working with them and they even had decent management. We tried to spread the good cheer further out west to get the home office to make the Elektrics a national priority, but things just didn't click.

Carole was obviously in another league. Her "Tapestry" album was iconic, and now with Capitol, she returned to the pearls in her publishing catalog. She did her own versions of "Up on the Roof," "Natural Woman," "Locomotion," "Chains," "Hey Girl" and more from the great Goffin/King song catalog.

She played out at Jones Beach. A perfect setting to hear those great songs by the beach.

Backstage she went out of her way to meet everyone. She posed for photos and signed albums and was the last to leave.

It seemed we were off to a great start, but the music failed to grab the attention of music directors throughout the land.

Carole was fantastic, but the album ended up being a dud.

Twenty-five years later I'd work with her again. It was a double live album called "The Living Room Tour." It was a hit! It debuted at #17 and was her biggest charting record since 1977.

Chapter 10

John Lennon 1980

I t was a boiling hot day and the sidewalks were siz-
zling. It was a summer afternoon in the Big Apple.
I was finishing up lunch over at Fontana Di Trivi,
an Italian restaurant across the street from Carnegie
Hall. The joint was the place Billy Joel was writing
about in "Scenes From An Italian Restaurant."

I was paying the bill when my friend, who was
looking out the front window, saw John Lennon
and said, "Dave, there's your friend." He was heading west on 57th Street. I caught up to him and two
guys, who I didn't know, who were walking with him.
Without missing a beat I had to say, "Hey John, how
do you get to Carnegie Hall?"

"Call the Rockefellers!" he said as he looked at
me. Then he asked, "Hey Dave, how are you? What
have you been doing? Is everything okay?"

I was holding on to his hand and didn't want to
let go. It was so great to see him. He had kinda just

disappeared for the past five years. There were no interviews or music or art or musings coming from him.

He told me he had new music he wanted to put out. I told him, "Great! I work at Capitol Records now!"

"They wouldn't listen to me then and I doubt they'll listen to me now. I've offered up ideas for artwork, but they don't get it," he pined.

I told him how great it was to see him and I'd be waiting to find out who he would sign with. Perhaps they would have an opening and I could get a chance to work his new record.

He was happy and nobody on 57th Street even stopped him besides me. I watched him until he was out of sight.

I felt lifted up and raring to go. John Lennon, in my book, was officially back in our arms.

Newsweek had an exclusive interview with Lennon that ran in September and brought us all up to date on everything John Lennon. In the middle of the month, Elton John played in Central Park, right outside John's window, and 400,000 people came. The show ran from 4 – 6 p.m. and we all thought for sure that John would play. You could feel the buzz. Elton made a reference about John, but he never appeared.

The first week of October came the official announcement in the trades. It said Geffen Records, in a worldwide deal, signed both Elton John and John & Yoko. Lennon's first work would be called "Double Fantasy."

We got more information the following week. "Starting Over" would be the first Lennon single in five years. It was coming out Friday, October 17th.

John's last single, "Stand By Me," hit #20 in 1975. The same year, "#9 Dream" reached #9. John's biggest solo single wasn't "Imagine" like most of us think. It was "Whatever Gets You Through The Night" back in 1974.

Meanwhile, in the UK, a weird event was taking place. Instead of the famous recording studio holding on to historic gear, EMI/Abbey Road studios held an auction to get rid of stuff. Believe it or not, they sold the 4-track-recording console used for the making of "Sgt. Peppers Lonely Hearts Club Band," and it went for only $1,200! Pathetic and a steal for a collector. Brian Epstein's book, "A Cellar Full of Noise," signed by all four Beatles sold for only $500. They also sold the mellotron used on "Strawberry Fields" for peanuts. A black day for Abbey Road, if you ask me. They should never have sold it.

It was not only great to see John making new music and being back on the scene, but now another press release came out saying Paul McCartney was working with George Martin again for the first time in five years since their big hit together called "Live and Let Die." Paul and George were working with a

40-piece orchestra on a movie Paul was doing on a favorite cartoon of his called "Rupert the Bear."

On December 7th, like I did each year, I went to my record collection and pulled out the Beatles "Yesterday & Today" Butcher cover that John had given to me to complete my Beatles record collection.

Besides his writing on the cover to me, he had torn off the back cover and made a drawing. Not a quick riff, but something thought out. It wasn't done quickly. I'd stare at it and wonder where he started to draw and what he was thinking. He even told me the drawing was rarer than the Beatles cover, but that I didn't understand that just yet.

He was gracious and warm to me. He was funny and soft-spoken. I remembered how he shook my hand and then gave it a little squeeze, like it was something special between us, and it was.

I would lie on my bed and hold this treasure and think, how did a kid like me ever get to meet his hero?

I met John back in '71 when he was in the studio with David Peel. David played in the parks in the Village and John saw how much he sounded like the Beatles when they began with their skiffel sound and were called the Quarrymen, named after their school.

Here it was 1980, and while reflecting on my early time with John, I noticed an ad for Peel's most recent record. I hadn't heard it, but it was called "John Lennon for President" and it was by David Peel and the Super Apple Band. Instead of Apple Records, he released it on Orange Records.

During that first week in December, the album, "Double Fantasy," came on the chart at 25*, the highest debut by any artist that week. The single, "Starting Over," was already top 10.

The opening line of the song was heartfelt and meaningful. "Our life together is so precious together."

Meanwhile, the last song on the album was "Hard Times Are Over." Yoko sang, "It's been very rough, but it's getting easier now, hard times are over, over for a while."

It brought me back to a song I promoted for Jennifer Warnes a few years earlier. She covered a Stephen Foster song called "Hard Times (Come Again No More)" that I'd listen to over and over. To me this was gospel music.

While I was thinking, I laid down and fell off to dreamland.

I was fast asleep when my phone rang. The caller told me John was dead.

He had been shot down in front of the Dakota, where he and Yoko lived.

It hit me like a 100 mile an hour fastball, straight in the gut. It stung me like a bee and knocked me to the floor. I was swarmed by bees. I was eaten alive with feelings. It was horrible. I woke up and my eyes were red and swollen from crying all night.

How could this be?

Hard times come around no more.

For the first time ever in my life, I wondered who I was, what I looked like, how old I was, where I was and what was I doing. Everything had gone by so quickly. Then I heard John's voice on the radio and it was different. I got chills and it hurt.

Nothing was ever the same again.

John was a true artist. 99% of the recording folks I worked with were not artists. They were just celebrities. John wrote, sang, painted and was a creative genius. He wrote "All You Need Is Love," "Give Peace A Chance," and "Imagine."

A few days later, on Sunday the 14th, there was a 10-minute silent mourning time in Central Park and in front of the Dakota building. It felt like 100,000 people had shown up. At exactly noon, it began to snow for the first time since last winter. "Listen The Snow Is Falling" by Yoko came into my mind. It was her finest moment and was the wonderful b-side to John's, "Happy Xmas (War Is Over)."

Chapter 11

Ricky Nelson

"C'mon Rick, we gotta go! It's almost 1:00 o'clock and we're due on the air in 30 minutes plus we still gotta grab a cab!" I pleaded.

Rick was wrapping up a newspaper interview when I knocked on his hotel door. The afternoon jock on WNEW begged me to bring him over, but it had to be before 2 p.m. when his air shift ended.

Rick thanked the reporter and showed him out the door. He then told me he'd be ready to go in a just a few moments. He disappeared into the bedroom while I waited. As we headed downstairs, I realized Rick was the most handsome man I ever worked with. He had movie star looks. He hair was perfect and he looked like he just got out of the barber's chair. His wore pants instead of jeans, his shirt was tucked in and he wore gold chains around his neck. He was definitely out of place for a rock leaning radio station where the jocks wore dungarees and t-shirts and kept aerosol cans of disinfectant in the studio. Rick even smelled good!

Rick was out promoting "Playing to Win," a super cool new rockabilly record he was working for Capitol Records. It was a terrific album that included songs from writers Ry Cooder, John Fogerty, Rosanne Cash, John Hiatt and Graham Parker. The album was a winner in my book! The great Jack Nitzsche produced it.

Time was tight but we made it to the radio station in time. Rick was in good spirits and the jock was well prepared. All was good.

After we said our goodbyes, Rick and I headed over to the country station further uptown. It had only been a matter of weeks since John Lennon was killed and Rick was uptight and on edge. Being in New York can only add to the tightness.

As we entered the country radio station, a man who was standing alone near the elevator rushed towards us and said, "Hey Rick!" Rick immediately thought he was a stalker and panicked. The floor was slippery and wet. He starting flailing his arms and then he slipped and fell down. It was like he was trying to get up from standing on a banana peel. As soon as Rick regained his footing, he pushed at the man to get out of his face and then he ran into the elevator. I put my arm out so no one else would enter. I had no idea how emotionally fragile Rick was that day. He was so far out of his comfort zone. When we left the station, we went out a side door in the case the guy who said hello was waiting for us.

Later that evening, Rick performed and was a true star. He was fantastic to all those he met. He took photos and signed some old album covers for fans.

Rick worked his album the hard way. He was doing many interviews on a show day. We all got behind him, but in the end the album just didn't break. It was his first and last album for Capitol, so I didn't have the opportunity to work with him again.

It was such a shock when he passed away in a terrible plane crash on the way to a New Year's Eve show in 1986.

Chapter 12

The Tubes

The Tubes were on tour and found themselves in Worchester, Massachusetts on a warm Saturday afternoon, preparing to do a radio interview followed by an in-store. Believe it or not, the radio station was inside a building called the Cocaine Realty Company. Our eyes lit up when we arrived.

Their new album was hilarious. They wanted it to turn your brain around so they called it "The Completion Backward Principal." Their new songs included the fun "Sushi Girl" and "Attack of the Fifty Foot Woman," plus their hit "Talk To You Later."

Fee, the lead singer, and I arrived around 1:45 p.m. As a promotion man, it's always tricky bringing an artist on the air during the weekend. It's the time the program directors put the part-timers on the air – the people that are working their way up the ladder. Usually the PD has to spend his weekend tuned in to the station and sometimes calling in to make adjustments.

On this afternoon, Fee arrived wanting to go right on the air. When we went into the studio, the jock put his hand out and told us what a big fan he was and how excited he was to be interviewing a band he followed. He immediately said to Fee, "Fay Weebill, it's so great to meet a man I admire so much! It's a quarter to the hour so let me finish this song, run some commercials and we'll start the interview at the top of the hour. How's that?" Fee piped back, "My name is Fee WAYBILL and I'm out of here at the top of the hour. Lets do this interview NOW!"

The station visit and the interview didn't go well, but the DJ did get a chance to mention the in-store down the block that would be starting soon. He told all the kids in Worchester to head down and pick up the new album and meet the band.

When we left the station, a kid from the record shop was out front. He told us to follow him to the store. He said there was a back entrance we should use, so we followed him.

I was the first inside the store. It was empty. It was either funny or awful depending on your mood. I was devastated. Fee felt like he was wasting his time doing all this promo shit.

I wondered how nobody could have shown up. "Where are the people?" I asked.

The man took me to the outside of the store and low and behold, behind a barrier were 200 kids waiting to scream and yell and steal records and get Fee's autograph.

The party was on!

Chapter 13

Muscle Shoals Sound Studios-
Sheffield, Alabama

I've been in some of the greatest recording studios during my career including Record Plant, Hit Factory, The Power Station, Electric Lady, Wally Heider's, Blue Rock, Abbey Road, RCA Studios in NY and Nashville and The Village Recorder in Los Angeles, but I always wanted to step inside the walls of Muscle Shoals Recording Studios in Alabama. The Rolling Stones had recorded there as well as Bob Dylan and Duane Allman.

It was 1981 and Capitol signed MSS Records. It stood for Muscle Shoals Sound Records. The folks in charge flew the Capitol staff down to hang out, get stoned, eat and listen to new music they'd been working on. We'd be hearing the music in one of the greatest studios ever.

I flew into Northwest Alabama Regional Airport and was picked up by a driver in a really fast Camaro. Within a nano second, he had a joint lit and passed it to me. It was a warm, beautiful evening.

Levon Helm from The Band was working on a solo album while we were there. Levon was down to earth and more than willing to share his stories and songs with us throughout our stay. Levon was a good ol' boy. Like an older brother. He'd been there and done it and survived. You could almost see the wounds of the road that had hardened him.

I shared a room with Stan from Seattle. Stan was the man. Stan always got more stations to add a single than any other Capitol promo man. When the boss quacked, "How many adds out of the box on blah blah blah are we gonna get?" Stan would say, "I'll have 10 adds!"

We got along great. Stan was a musician prior to becoming a promotion man, so he knew his way around recording artists better than anyone.

The town is dry, so the next morning Stan and I drove miles to the nearest liquor store to get some booze. Once we scored, we headed to eat breakfast. Stan opened the fruit jar of hooch and poured some into his orange juice. Immediately it started to bubble.

"Is it supposed to do that?" I asked.

"Shit man, I've never seen that before!" he barked. "Over the teeth and past the gums, look out stomach, here it comes!" he blurted.

I saw his head turn red and his eyes popping out. I handed him my napkin to wipe the sweat coming off him.

"Jesus! That's got a kick like a mule!"

Stan ran to the bathroom. After 15 minutes, I asked for the check and went to find Stan.

Driving back to the studio, I saw the cop car and then I heard the siren. We were getting pulled over.

SHIT!

We're alone on a rural highway in Alabama and we've got open containers of booze reeking in the backseat on the floor.

I was feeling queasy.

However, after the fear subsided, we kicked into our skills as promotion men and told the cop we were down here to have fun over at the studio. He was cool! I was carrying my Polaroid™ camera and he took a photograph of Stan and I by the squad car with our hands behind our backs.

We finally went over to the studio and spent the rest of the day meeting all the new label guys and listening to music. Jerry Wexler, the great producer from Atlantic Records, was there too. This was a very big deal to us. We loved his work and now we were getting a chance to know the man who produced many of the records we loved the most. He had done the Wicked Pickett down here and Aretha Franklin too. Artist Lou Ann Barton was recording an album for Asylum and Jerry Wexler was producing the sessions with Glenn Frey, who was fresh off the break-up of the Eagles. Frey also recorded part of his debut solo album, "No Fun Aloud," at Muscle Shoals.

When we arrived for dinner and learned Jerry would be joining us, we ran to sit right down next to him. We had our bottle of Everclear 180 proof booze. When Jerry saw what we were drinking, he promptly told us, "We clean the tape heads with that shit. Be careful drinking it!"

We really kicked it back down here. There was no stress. No phones ringing, no messages to return, but plenty of drugs and private stash booze to keep us locked down good and tight. But all too soon, we'd be back in our offices, with the rumpdog boss barking at our heels.

Chapter 14

Spiffs For Stiffs

The Capitol Records promo bosses used indies to get their records played. They spent a ton of money on a ton of stiffs. The release schedule was always full and they didn't want to lose a hit, so they started singles with the indies, who were now grossly overpaid. Even regional artists were getting a shotgun effect with small pockets of airplay all over the country.

Having worked top 40 in New York City, I knew the indies had no juice whatsoever. WABC was a corporate station that had strict rules and rarely took calls from an outside independent. Perhaps if a guy who they knew was out of a job they would let him stop by, but that was rare.

Most label promotion folks were making a good living with a salary and an expense account but nothing close to the $80 million a year the indies were raking in from major labels.

The Capitol staff would do a full investigation on each record at every station they were responsible for and feed back the information to the home office. Instead of beating dead horses or singles that showed no fire power, we'd concentrate on getting to number one with the proven hits we did have.

Rather than tell the artist their song was a dud, the head of promotion would hire and overpay the indies to show management and executive staff there was a story building. This is where the bullshit began.

There were a bunch of tiny privately-owned radio stations. These small stations often changed formats and didn't pay much if you worked there. Somebody, way back when, decided to accumulate a list of these small radio stations, many whom weren't even on a list to get free singles, and began to call them. These were stations that were in towns you couldn't spell and none of the places had airports. They were way out in the boondocks with weak radio signals. Someone figured if you could get 10 of these pee wee radio stations to add a record at the same time, it could come on a chart they would call 'bubbling under,' which meant the record wasn't on the top 100 of *Billboard*. This was the easiest job in the world. These pee wee stations could and would play 60 records. But in most cases, there was no printed playlist and these new songs they added would either never be played or be played overnight or played so infrequently they would only be heard in the overnights.

Think of it this way. If you and me were truck drivers and you drove during the day and I drove the overnight shift, we'd both be hearing different songs on the same station. The PDs would stick new music on the overnight shift and then hope it would be a hit so they could play it during the daytime hours.

As one would guess, these overnight songs rarely sold or got any requests, but the guy that got in on 10 stations could charge good money to tell a record company "it looks like you may have a hit you don't even know about." This was catnip to a boss who wanted to get new records on to radio stations.

Many of the indies typed up a fake playlist and showed the song at let's say, #50, even though a station wasn't playing 50 records. The indie would get paid for that add. The following week, the indie would type out the fake list and show it moving 50 to 43 and then they would get paid for the upward movement, too. This bonus was called a "spiff."

At this juncture, the sales people would start to pay attention and make sure there were copies in store. The press department would go to the secondary markets and try to get some action in the newspapers. The A&R department would already be thinking of the next single and telling the band

and manager how great things were looking. Venues that were contacted were now interested in booking a show, which would mean a possible tour to support this new-fangled success. Everything was in play except knowing if it was a legitimate hit or just paper adds that were fueled by money.

The label's promotion department would take over the momentum and try to get it played on the biggest stations in the biggest markets. They were told to deliver at any cost. Whether it was free cases of Beatle albums, autographs, guitars, tickets, etc. This just fueled the bullshit in the home office that we may have a hit, however, there was no real information to indicate the record was a hit. It wasn't getting played heavy, it was being played in markets no one ever heard of, there were no requests from people wanting to hear it, and there was no feedback from a record store that there were any records selling.

This is the kind of situation that can make grown promotion people cry. Most of those indie records never made it. As Stevie Wonder once wrote and sang, "Just because a record has a groove don't make it in the groove."

When it was time to take out the big full-page ads and go after the big market radio stations, the record companies would find out fast that the road ahead was going to be tough.

It was at this critical moment the VP of promotion always took the wrong fork in the road. He believed in his own hype. He was sucking his own fumes. The reality was these were never hit records by any means, but that didn't stop the rumpdog from screaming at you to deliver your top station. They would yell at you so loud and so often, making people cry and feel insecure. In my case, dealing with the toughest radio stations in the biggest market, I knew none of these indies could do any damage since the stations would never fall for the hype. These top stations were paying a fortune for their own research, which certainly was different from what promotion people were feeding them.

Capitol went way to0 far on a stiff like the band Prism. It's a great example of how fucked the boss could get when he wanted to believe his indies could get records played and made into hits while he treating his staff like they knew nothing.

Prism was a Canadian rock band with members we never heard of. They had no history and never toured in America. There was no story to run with. It was an average record. You don't just wave a finger and put 50 adds on the board with this work record. The album was viewed negatively by the majority of music critics. It was also a commercial disappointment, failing to chart on the *Billboard* 200.

The boss wanted it treated like a new Beatles record!

When this rant went on and I had to listen to it even on weekends and at nights, I came up with a new way to describe it. I called the yellers and screamers rumpdogs.

You could smell the rump or rear end of these dogs from 3,000 miles away.

Chapter 15

The Beatles-A Taste of Honey-March 28, 1982

It was a Sunday evening and I was beat. It had been a long week and I just wanted to veg out and watch whatever the 8pm movie was coming on TV, but when you work in the music business, there is no rest.

The boss figured he'd beat us up from Beverly Hills. It was three hours earlier on the West Coast, so he could get us out of the way and head out in his Rolls Royce for dinner with some arm candy.

It was early in Los Angeles and late in New York. This is no way to spend a Sunday evening at home.

My phone rang and I was in no mood for coffee or a glass of wine. I knew I couldn't zone out on this nut.

The rumpdog was on the phone having a conniption! He wanted "I'll Try Something New" by A Taste Of Honey to break at Pop radio and he was absolute in his screaming fit. He did NOT want the Beatle record to beat it.

"Alright! This is a much needed phone call!!!

"There are a lot of negatives to go over and you've really got to get organized!

"There are a lot of things that disturb me!!!

"Some people really need to be put in line!!

"I'm sick and tired of the radio programmers telling me we don't have the product!! They say we don't have the kind of records we can excel in!! They say we don't have the heavyweights!!! They say we don't have records we can cross over!!!!!

"Now let me get down to what's bothering me. I made a commitment on behalf of this staff. I said this is gonna be the year we take R&B records and cross them over!!! I don't mean MAIL THE RECORDS TO THE STATIONS!!! We're gonna make hits out of them!!!

"I'm going to spend money on the independents!! I'm gonna wheel and deal until we make hits out of them!!!

"Now I guess the average person sitting there would say, A Taste of Honey's 'I'll Try Something New' is in no trouble. It's rolling along at #50 with a bullet in *Cashbox* but the idea that everything is jolly is fuckin' GARBAGE!!! It's not jolly!!! We got six fucking adds last week!!! And this is our #1 PRIORITY!! This record is being mistreated by this awful staff!!!!

"It's BULLSHIT!!!

"It's OUTRAGEOUS!!!!

"We hit the fucking brick wall thanks to you assholes!!!

"Now this is a joke! If we blow this record we're FUCKED!!! This is the only avenue of revenue we have this year!!! Now this record is in deep trouble!!!

"Who's blowing this fucking record??? YOU ARE!! You're blowing this hit record! Why?? Because YOU think I'm gonna do the work!!! You think the OTHER GUY is gonna do the work!!! You think the independents are going to do YOUR work!!!! You think you don't have to worry about it until I beat you over the fucking head with it!!!!!

"I got a Beatles record ("Beatles Movie Medley"), but I say FUCK THE BEATLES!!!!

"I got a Little River Band ("Man On Your Mind") but I say FUCK THEM TOO!!!

"You jerks just figure you can phone in a few adds on these two records and then go hide for a couple of weeks!!!! Well, I'm gonna fuck you up and beat you right now!!!

"It's the #1 fucking priority and if we lose the Taste of Honey you better get out of Capitol Records!!!!!

"These records don't run on their own steam. Hit records don't just happen! They're made by the promotion staff!!!

"Now the manager of A Taste Of Honey calls me up and says he's having a party at his house to congratulate the promotion staff. I WOULDN'T GO TO THE FUCKING PARTY!!! You know why??? I was fucking embarrassed!!!! I'm ashamed of the job being done on this record!!!

"Come hell or high water, you better figure this out!!!!

"You gotta deliver!!!

"Six fucking adds? Six out of 100 radio stations?? THAT'S BULLSHIT!!! It's horrible and I'm embarrassed!!! Now I gotta go to the trades and beg them for a fucking bullet next week!!!!

"I want you out there next week scraping up a few bandit stations! The kind that will add ANYTHING!!!

"Where the fuck is the Capitol promotion staff???? They're out there GETTING THE BEATLES PLAYED!!!! Well, what the fuck are we gonna do with the Beatles????? This is a one-off wham bam thank you, good fucking bye, see ya later alligator record!!!!!!

"You better get out there and wheel and deal!!! MANEUVER!!! I hope you understand me. You suck! You only work the easy stations. You can't bring it home!!

"I want 20 adds next week!!! I thought we were big boys who could deliver!!!!

"If you can't deliver one small station, one medium station, and one big station, I'm taking the money OUT OF YOUR PAYCHECKS AND PUTTING ON INDEPENDENTS IN YOUR MARKET!!!

"I'm very nervous. I don't know what else to do!!!!!

"You better deliver adds!!!! I don't care if it's a FAVOR!!! I don't care if it's a FAKE PAPER ADD!!! I don't care if it's a REAL ADD!!!! I don't care if it's an add with a number!!!! I don't care if you give away a ton of Beatles albums!!!! GET THE JOB DONE!!!

"Let's move on to Prism. It's the #1 rock song. "Turn On Your Radar" is the single and it's coming Monday. It's the #2 priority so I want you to go out and chase it at pop stations like you're running with the hottest Beatles record!!! If this isn't a fucking hit record, I don't know what it is!!! This is a total pop smash!! Everyone says it's a hit!!!! We got a shot now to break this group! You have to bust them wide open!!! We have a smash single!!! NOBODY CAN SAY IT ISN'T!!!! We got the staff! We got the money behind it! We got it all going!!!! SURE, there's a Paul McCartney record out there ("Ebony and Ivory" w/ Stevie Wonder), SO WHAT!!! He'll take up a slot, but you know something? There's plenty of other spots!!! Remember, Prism has a damn good reputation and a tremendous base!!! It's a new record and I expect impact! We should have three strong weeks with this record right out of the box!!! There's not a thing we're are not prepared to do for this record!!!! THIS HAS TO BE A POP HIT!!!

"Okay, we gotta move on to Ashford and Simpson's "Street Corner." This is the song we gotta break! We

PROMISED them a big career with Capitol Records. I've heard this record 25 times and I stood up and made a commitment to this record. I told them this will be a pop priority right out of the box. I'm after it!!! I'm swinging!!! And I'm paying spiff money to the independents!!!!! It's a fucking HOME RUN!!!

"Alright. Next. We're putting out a record strictly for radio. It's not for sale. We signed a west coast group called Missing Persons and they got a little record called "Words." Get it around. Let's see what happens.

"If I sound panicked or impatient it's because the pressure is ON! I don't care if they are hype records! Get them on the radio!!!!

"Also, on April 12, you'll get "Only The Lonely" by the Motels. We have put a colossal amount of money behind this project. It's our biggest commitment since Juice Newton!! You're going to see two-page color ads in the trades. We're going with high-grade vinyl and servicing radio with a special cassette, an improved expanded range Dolby tape which shows our huge commitment! We'll also be servicing photographs and lyric sheets. We've waited a year and a half to create this huge roll-out and it's going to require effort! It's Capitol's favorite act! The President of the label said, 'We're going to cash in!!! We are committed as we were for Bob Seger!' We all want a blitz effort! Do all you have to do! You guys get it played and we will support you!!!

"Two weeks later we're coming with the new Juice Newton.

"Okay, now listen to me. I want you out at the clubs at night!!! Go to the goddamn clubs and get wired to the owner who puts the videos on the screens. We want our videos up on that fucking screen! The fucking Go-Go's, Soft Cell, Human League all SUCK! Get our artists played!!"

Ray, the VP of rock promotion, then took over the call and said:

"Finally, on the rock side, Iron Maiden is the priority! Rock stations are open for night airplay. We'll back this up with time buys, so go after features and weekend tests. "Number of the Beast" is the album. Iron Maiden is a legit act with huge sales! We will be very aggressive. There is a new lead singer, Bruce Dickinson, and Martin Birch, who did the early Black Sabbath records, produced the music. The new track "Run to the Hills" is the most successful heavy metal single ever in Britain. The band will be here in six weeks for a four-month tour with .38 Special and Rainbow."

When it was all over, "The Beatles Movie Medley" went to #12, while A Taste Of Honey stalled at #41, never allowing it to reach the respectable top 40 chart in *Billboard*. It was no "Boogie Oogie Oogie," their No. 1 hit from the late 70s.

Chapter 16

"It's Do or Die!"

The smell of the rumpdog was in my nose. These calls never stopped. They were never good. You walked away from the phone not wanting to work. They weren't inspirational, go-get-'em-team kinda calls. They were vile.

The phone was ringing and I had to pick it up. It was the boss.

I took out a sheet a paper to take notes. I wrote the date at the top of the page. It was April 18, 1982.

"This week Prism should have had 20 fuckin' adds!!! It's a formula single for fuck's sake!!!! Now I gotta stop the train to save this record!!!

"The Motels were supposed to come roaring in with a substantial amount of adds and we come on by the skin of our teeth at #90 with a bullet!!!! NO FUCKING IMPACT!!!! This is where the Mickey Mouse records go!!!! Nobody takes #90 with a bullet seriously!!!!! I AM SO PISSED!!! This is like a record on RCA that comes on at #90 and goes to #80 and then you never hear of it again!!!

"SO NOW WE'RE FUCKED!!!

"We're backed up!!! I carefully planned to put out the Juice Newton knowing we'll have two good weeks with two strong records!!! I was going to close them like a good Neil Diamond record!!!

"When they told me the goddamn Juice Newton record had a problem with mastering, you know what I said? 'THANK GOD, WE BOUGHT A WEEK'S TIME!!!'

"Now how the fuck ya gonna do it all??? You gonna THINK about it???

"You're all gonna have to face me in Palm Springs in a few days!!!!! The PRESIDENT is gonna walk up to you and say, 'What the fuck is going on?'

"If we lose these records, it's gonna be a house of horrors down there!!!! I'm not looking forward to ten hours a day of this fuckin' shit!!!!!

"You're not hustling!!!!

"You're NOT FUCKING TRYING!!!

"You're like the New York Knicks where everybody is an All-Star!!! Everybody is the best in their market, but you can't win!!!!!! YOU'RE EMBARRASSING!!!!!!

"We're gonna break Prism!!!!!! You fuckin' idiots better get four cockamamie stations!!!!!

"This was the single that was gonna make Prism HAPPEN!!!!!!

"What about the Motels???? I told you to GO FOR THE THROAT and what did you get???? ZERO!!!! We're two weeks behind!!!!! RCA can do it!! Look at Lighthouse!! They ran it up the flagpole!!!!!

"I should have put the independents on AT ANY PRICE TO INSURE MY BET!!!!

"Everyone at the Tower feels the same way!!!

"They whisper to me, 'What's happening? What happened? What's going on????'

"You put yourself against the wall!!!!!!

"Now there's no way I'm going to the convention in Palm Springs and have a good time!!!

"BULLSHIT!!!

"It's gonna be work!!!! Like working for IBM…….. NO FUN!!!!

"It's do or die!!!

"If we blow Prism, we blow a fortune!!!! It's #79 with a bullet and I am running out of favors!!!!

"That's IT!
GOOD NIGHT!"

Chapter 17

Palm Springs Pep Talk

Wow. I was just getting warmed up at Capitol when the boss told us we were heading to Palm Springs for a company convention. This sounded great. I'd never been. I'd get to meet all the other promotion folks and people from the Tower in Hollywood.

I started to find out about the town. Palm Springs, California is a desert town and in April it gets to 90 degrees with no humidity. In the evening, it's a very pleasant 65 degrees. I was thinking about those old movies where doctors used to tell their stressed out patients to "head to the desert, relax, you'll feel better."

The last time I traveled so far out west was at a Warner Bros. Records convention in Camelback, Arizona back in '75. We arrived at this desert oasis and did nothing but lay at the pool and get to know each other. The hardest activity was lifting a beer. During the convention, WB presented us with all new talent. We met and hung out with Emmylou Harris and Al Jarreau. It was incredible and, if I close my eyes, I can see Emmylou performing by the pool right now. The memory is forever.

At most record companies, we'd talk to the boss on a regular basis and once in a while have a conference call. At Capitol, there always seemed to be conference calls. I once met a woman who told me she would cry at the cruel way they would speak to the staff. She told me that one day, she ran out of her room and her mother picked up the phone and went ballistic on the man running the call.

At Capitol, I was very lucky. I was the east coast rock guy, so I never got yelled at by the top 40 guy. I was now officially out of the top 40 game and happy to be working exclusively with the key rock stations.

Ray, my rock department boss, was a mellow guy. I never ever heard him raise his voice. We were cool. We understood each other. When Ray would come to New York, he never went to a radio station. He had everyone come meet him in his hotel room. Ray had it together big time. He'd have the champagne chilled, the best coke, the best pot, and he'd have a stereo hookup that was out of this world. He'd call downstairs and have the hotel sound man come up with ballroom, convention size speakers. He also made sure he was put as far away as other guests as possible. Once you were in Ray's room, you didn't want to leave. Most folks walked in and didn't leave until Ray left town a day or two later.

Meanwhile, the top 40 guy was what I call a rump-dog. You could smell these guys over a phone. In this particular case, the guy was from New York and grew up with the same radio stations I grew up with. If he was in the music business as a radio promotion man, he sure must have known how difficult it was to get records added to WABC, the tightest and toughest radio station in all the land with the biggest ratings of anyone. Not to mention you could hear them all the way to Florida, if you tried.

The head of promotion should be a leader, a mentor to help you reach your goals. When you're in trouble, they should pick up the phone and place a call to the radio station, too. Obviously, they should know the music, but I found that was not the case. Most guys would spend a half hour screaming about a song and never mention the title. Most times they never knew who the artist was.

My mind was 100% on the upcoming journey to the desert town of Palm Springs but, while I was packing, the Capitol promo chief decided to have a conference call. He wanted to get us ready for what we could expect.

I heard the phone ring and when I picked it up, I could smell the other end of the line. A rumpdog was speaking and the odor was rancid.

"All right let's get right into it. I just want to say straight out, up front, I don't know what's happening to this promotion staff! We're being out-promoted and we're becoming the laughing stock out there! I don't know what's happening to this staff. I don't know what's happening to the direction, but something has really gone wrong.

"Now, we set up priorities, we build projects, we do things, and nobody gives a shit! Everybody thinks it's just going to go by itself and there's no follow through, no blitz, and it's really becoming apparent. We really have to knock some heads and this isn't just coming from me. It's coming from everybody upstairs! We are really getting out-promoted, out crushed every week for the last few weeks. It's a joke!!

"Polydor is running us off the field, RCA's been kicking our ass for a year every week, killing us. Now those guys are pumped up, fired up, doing it! They're hungry and we're not, it's apparent!!

"We're like a team that won the pennant, like the Dodgers, and we're fat. We're sitting back and we're lazy, we're like the Philadelphia Phillies, we suck! That's what we are. A lot of big names, a lot of hot dogs, a lot of big stars in the market. Nobody's working their ass off anymore. Nobody's delivering like they used to!!

"Why is it that we start to build things and then drop the ball?

"I got caught with my ass out there with a hit record and the rest of you guys didn't deliver. I'm embarrassed. What the fuck is going on out there?!!!

"Now I want to review a few things and I wanna give you guys some very lovely things that are gonna happen in Palm Springs that I've got all prepared for you.

"We have this lovely trip planned for Palm Springs. The President made up an agenda. It's very nice, he took care of you guys. Monday morning is free. You can play tennis, sit around the pool 'til 2 o'clock, have lunch, take the rest of the day off. Same thing for Tuesday. Individual meetings with promo guys at 2 o'clock, mornings off, play tennis, shoot a round of golf, free evenings, and so on and so forth.

"Well, I said to the President, I would like to revise this whole agenda, and he said, 'what's the matter?' I said, 'I'll tell you what's the matter. I need more time. I need more than from 2 o'clock to whatever. I need from 9 o'clock in the morning till 6 o'clock at night, every day!'

"Every single day to do what?" the President asked.

"To do the basics. To go over and over and over like an army drill instructor! How to promote a record for starters! We'll do it one on one, with each guy and then at night!

"Where it says nights are free, you're not gonna be free, 'cause I'm going to schedule you by groups to come into my room, 'cause we're gonna go over how to promote a record. Station by station, city by city, town by town, person by person!

"I don't give a shit about Palm Springs. I've got a beautiful house down there, I go down there so many times. It's 80 degrees in Los Angeles today. Imagine how beautiful it's going to be when you guys get down there. You wanna sit in the sun, try to grab a tan. No tan this year, nobody's gonna have any fun!! You're going to be in meetings from 9 'til 6!! We're gonna feed you and then have you on standby for more seminars!! We're gonna sit there and I'm gonna break it down until we get back on the fucking ball!!!

"Now if you don't want that, and you wanna have a good time, let me tell you how to have a good time. You can become mad again, you can become fighters again, you can stop letting shitty records like Rainbow and guys I never heard of, thousands of records, beat us!!!!

"Now, this is what I'm pissed off about!!! I go to *Billboard* to see the chart editor, he says I'm going to give you a bullet on Prism but how 'bout getting some airplay?!!!!

"I told you Prism was a priority!!

"It's 79 with a bullet!! That sucks!! Last week everyone went south on the record. I'm looking down at the airplay we got. Portland, Corpus Christi, Lansing, and a station in Columbia, Missouri. That's the blitz? Do any of you look at your stats, scratch your heads and say what are the rest of the guys doing!!!

"This was supposed to be the big follow up. This is the act we're gonna break. We got the quote 'Turn on Your Radar' THE ROCK & ROLL POP SINGLE OF THE YEAR!!!

"We said we'd get 20 adds out of the box, which we didn't get!!!

"We said we're gonna come right back with 30 adds the next week!!!!

"What do we get? Four fucking stations!!! FOUR STATIONS!!!!!!

"This is Capitol Records, this is supposed to be the best promotion men, the giants, the heaviest guys in the business and Polydor got more adds on an act I never heard of, and their boss hasn't done promotion for five years. In fact, he hasn't done promotion in twenty-five years and he got more adds. It's embarrassing. It's an insult!!!!!!!!!"

Now the rumpdog focused his rant on the Motels.

"Now we go out and we say we're going to do a massive job on the Motels and we come up with 10 stations!!!! Which, I don't want to tell you too much of my business, but I would say a good proportion of those adds were from an independent promotion man who said to me, 'Hey you had a great week, didn't you?' 'Yeah,' I said, 'I came in 90 with a bullet, and I got two stations you didn't get! Then he said to me, 'What the hell's the matter with your staff? They really dropped the ball!' Now that was downright embarrassing!!"

Now the rumpdog talked about the crossover R&B records that peaked and were ready for possible top 40 airplay.

"Forget the black records we lost, I won't even mention Taste of Honey, which is history. I won't mention it's a record that's over 200,000, that we're not gonna take any further 'cause nobody went out and did their killer spread with their pop stations!!!! I've already flushed it down the toilet!!

"But I will not accept Prism and Motels dribbling and squirming!!! If I were a program director and you came to me next week and said, 'Prism is my priority,' I'd laugh at you.

"It's gonna take $50,000 with independents this week to get the record off its ass so you'll have enough goddamn stations to go in with 20 stations next week!!!!!

"I'm livid!! I can't believe that you've blown a Prism record!!!! What were you going to do next week? Get three or four adds and hope that I send my right hand guy to *Billboard* to bend over and blow the guy for a bullet again!!!! Damn it! Do I gotta go over to the home of the *Billboard* Chart editor and do a tap dance?

"Independents are laughing at us. They say we suck!!!!"

Dave Morrell

After banging his hand down hard and me wishing it was his head, he continued with all the other priorities.

"I'm gonna talk about Little River Band single 'Man On Your Mind!' I'm gonna take the stats and look at them right fucking now!!! In New York, there's a hole! Chicago, there's a hole! Miami hole! Boston, Boston is a fucking embarrassment!!!! I would crawl under a rock if I lived in Boston!! There isn't even a middle of the road station playing the fucking thing there!!!! Detroit, NOTHING! Minneapolis NOTHING! Dallas NOTHING!!!! This is Little River Band, 42 with a super bullet, coming off two top ten records in a row!!!! We got major holes!!! I can see us begging and screaming in two weeks to get Little River Band played.

"I'm excited about the Missing Persons record, which is about 30,000 sold in Los Angeles already, but I can't get crazy because Little River Band isn't even closed out in this town!!!

"I wanna talk about Missing Persons! I wanna talk about Jay Ferguson! I wanna talk about Ashford & Simpson, which is already 24 on the black charts!!! But I can't because I'm being stymied and held back since I can't get Prism and the Motels played!!!

"We're in very big trouble!! The Motels came on with horrible impact!! It's 90 with a bullet!! 90 with a bullet!!!!! I'm so embarrassed I don't even want it to be on. I wish I could go back and have them take it off the chart!!! This is the real Capitol crush? 90 with a bullet?

"We go for the knockout punch and we fall flat on our ass. We come up with nothing. What do we got? 5% of the country to show for it!! Two hundred stations and we come up with ten? I think the ten could go on by itself without even sending you guys in!!! It's horrible, it's just fucking horrible, it's embarrassing!!!

"I had to do such a tap-dance with the President upstairs! I gave him the stroke *Billboard* numbers and I shuffled him off!!! I can't do it next week! We're not going to get a bullet if we have a lousy week like last week!!!!!

"I think we should take everybody and drill them, and shit on them, until they drop and die of heat exhaustion in Palm Springs!!!

"I swear I'm not kidding you!!!

"I'm prepared to sit in those goddamn cold rooms with the orange juice and water and go over the fundamentals of getting up in the morning and brushing your teeth and what you have to do!!! I'll do a goddamn manual on it all over again because somewhere along the lines, nobody cares anymore. The killer instinct is gone.

"We're too easy on you. The only way I can get pissed off is when your quarterly reviews come around and I put 'unsatisfactory' with airplay. That's what I'll start doing. It'll cost you a few dollars.

"I've been doing nothing all weekend but wining and dining two of the biggest indies in the business!!! Spending money and filling their pockets. I don't care if they know the band or have heard the goddamn song!!! I've been badgering them for days because I'm so scared that you guys aren't gonna be able to deliver enough to keep these records alive. You're all a joke to me!!!

"Now am I out of my mind not to think the Motels is in serious trouble? It's being blasted at rock radio! It's being acclaimed by everybody as a fabulous record! Capitol Records is totally committed with two-page color ads in the trades! We're backing up all our effort, and I come up with 10 adds, of which, the independent got the majority of them and you know it when you look at your markets!!! So, I'm very disgusted with the job done, no impact at all for this shit staff! You came up with nothing!!!

"We can't work two records at once. Two major important records.

"Now the reason I'm really upset, besides really blowing Prism and Motels, is Thursday you will be receiving an absolute #1 record by Juice Newton, 'Loves Been a Little Bit Hard on Me'. My key man has played it for program directors and they all said, 'Absolute smash! Home run!'

"But my problem with this record is that when it comes out, it will run on its own, and I'll get knocked out of the box because my staff can't get airplay on the ones ahead of it, Prism and Motels!!!

"This staff can't juggle and think ahead and be all set up!!!!

"If you think it's funny, great!!! You won't think it's funny when you're in Palm Springs, 'cause I swear to you, I'm not letting up!!! I really think we need to sit down, look everybody in the eye and start picking each other apart and getting on each other because this is NO JOKE!

"We're gonna sit in those cold conference rooms all day while it's 80 degrees and gorgeous outside!!!

"Don't bring your tennis racquet, don't bring your bathing suit, save the space in your luggage, you won't need it. Bring a pair of blue jeans and a T-shirt and a couple of neckerchiefs to wipe your brow because it's gonna get hot in those rooms. That's all you're gonna need, plus a soft pair of shoes 'cause you aren't going anywhere. Don't bring any suntan lotion. You won't need it.

"Pain in the ass, the whole thing's a fucking joke to all of you!!!

"Well I'm thoroughly disgusted I have to stoop to this shit to get my records played.

"Good fucking night!"

And then the phone went silent.

I didn't want to go to Palm Springs anymore. Before I got up to go to the bathroom my phone was ringing. For the next hour, I fielded calls from the pissed off local promotion team. Some were even crying.

I was one year into a long drawn out decade at Capitol that would find many other heads of promotion taking the same route – screaming at people who were doing their best.

There was no rest.

Chapter 18

Capitol Records Rock Man

While we were getting beat up down in Palm Springs, we did manage to have a respectable dinner where a few people were recognized for their good work.

They gave out pins for people that had five years of experience and called each one up to the stage. Then they gave out awards for top 40 and R&B promotion people. Then came the unexpected.

"Dave Morrell is our Rock Promotion Manager of the Year!"

I'd been at Capitol for a year now, busting my rump, and was so thankful they recognized my ability to work with others and get records played on radio stations. Getting this award in front of the staff was important. The old-timers realized I was now a real part of the Capitol team. I knew they'd return my phone calls, take action when needed, and be reliable when we had to work together. On a national level, I knew all the people at the Tower would now hear about me and welcome me when I visited. Back on my home turf, the award meant nothing. Those already working with me didn't care one iota.

I was just hoping to get back to Palm Springs soon so I could actually enjoy it!

The convention didn't go off without a major fuck up. *Billboard* even picked up on it.

The story said, "Frank Turner, 41, longtime Atlanta promotion man, was arrested last week at the Sheraton Oasis Hotel, Palm Springs, for possession of narcotics by the Palm Springs police. Turner was in the hotel as record company employees were holding a national meeting. He's out on $5,000 bail. According to police, they found cocaine, Quaaludes, and marijuana in his hotel room. He will be arraigned in the next seven to ten days. If convicted, he could face imprisonment for state law violation. According to a Capitol Records source, Turner has resigned from his Atlanta position since the arrest."

We all left the convention with our heads down. It was a dark day on a cloudless, 80-degree afternoon in sunny, beautiful Palm Springs.

Ten years later, back in Palm Springs, the cops would be coming again. They were after the new head of promotion for exposing himself. It was ugly but it didn't make the news.

Chapter 19

"You Better Turn It Around Fast!!!"

You could feel the tension in your body before the weekly conference call started. You just knew it was going to be a mental beating. I grabbed a sharp pencil and a fresh sheet of paper.

Most of the jabbing was at the top 40 team, but you couldn't help but feel for them.

"For fuck's sake, what the hell is going on out there!!" Mr. Rolls Royce snarled. "April Wine has given us three albums and now we're battling with this group!! Fuck! We now have them in the Platinum category, but you took them for granted! You thought it would take care of itself!! The radio people think we don't care!! They think we don't bust our ass!! They think we're jerking around!!! 'Enough Is Enough' is a smash!! Let's fucking close it! I don't wanna hear any problems!

"We gotta maneuver the Frankie Miller song 'To Dream The Dream.' This is our blitz commitment record! We came on Billboard at #81!! If Bob Seger sang this fucking song, we'd have 98% of radio on board!!!

"On 'Street Corner' by Ashford and Simpson, I have shouted and talked about it!! It's a top 10 **R&B** record and it's our job to cross it over to top 40!!!! I want it worked at all your stations! We owe it to ourselves!!! I don't see anyone working it, for fuck's sake!!! What are we doing???? You tell me!!!!

"I'm getting annoyed now!!!!

"We haven't kicked ass on Missing Persons!!! I'm dedicated to breaking this record!!! You know what? Even the fucking hard nose radio people are telling me it's a smash!!!! Move your ass and get some adds! We're at 70,000 units on the EP!!!

"A few people on the staff like Duran Duran's 'Hungry Like The Wolf.' Let's try to keep the fuckin' thing alive. Try to create a buzz. Try to find an opening. If radio asks, tell them we're working it but remember, we are congested!!!! Do NOT let this record get in our way if you know what I mean!!! We got three ballbuster records and we're loaded at the top, so who knows about the Duran Duran.

"All right!! Now let's not forget Mel McDaniel's 'Big Ole Brew.' It's a fuckin' smash at Country radio stations. It's gonna be a #1 Country record!!! This means sales!!!! I've allotted a ton of fuckin' money to make this a crossover smash!! All the independents are IN!! I want to bust ass and make this a fuckin' pop hit record!!!

"Now listen up! I'm headed to a convention next week and I don't want to walk in without hits!!! I don't want nobody buggin' me in the lobby about how come we can't break records!!!!!!! You better turn it around fast!!!"

Chapter 20

The Jordanaire

By complete surprise, I ran into a kid named Hylton Hawkins. He worked in Nashville for Capitol and at some event we said hello to each other. We hit it off pretty well and went to smoke a joint. While we were blowing smoke rings, he told me his father was a Jordanaire who backed up Elvis Presley, among others.

He said his old man was sick in the hospital. It hit that spot we all have inside of us. I told him a friend of mine had some kinescope films of Elvis on "The Ed Sullivan Show" with the Jordanaires backing up the King. I told him it was rare and my friend and I were hoping to show it to John Lennon some day. I wondered if his dad had stuff like this in his collection. He didn't.

Hylton called his mother and she was so happy she cried. Her name was Dorothy Jean, but they called her Dotty, and she said she was backstage at the moment Elvis hit the stage and so she never saw it on television. I called my friend and asked him politely to fly down to Nashville with 16mm prints so we could show it in the hospital for the old man. I told him it was a mission of mercy. He wasn't going to get paid and he'd have to pick up his own expenses plus, somehow, find a 16mm projector. I told him he could stay at the Hawkins' home.

The day came and there we were in Nashville in Hoyt Hawkins' hospital room. He didn't look too good and he had tubes in his nose, so saying anything was impossible for him. I was hoping for a miracle for this good man.

When we started up the machine, a few nurses came in to see what was happening.

We turned it on and we turned up the volume.

And then Elvis appeared on the screen!

It was spectacular. The old man started crying and gripping his wife's hand. She was crying too.

As the King was swinging and rocking and rolling, the Jordanaires were snapping their fingers and singing beautiful harmonies. This was historic at the time it was shown live. It was very emotional to be in the room with the family now and see how they were clearly shaken with goodness and love and joy and happiness against the backdrop of a young man and his father, who was lying on his back, unable to speak.

When it was over, we all sobbed and then his wife Dotty spoke.

She told us how she put on Elvis' makeup before he went on the stage on that fateful evening. She said she still had the powder and the puffer back at her house and she would show it to us later.

I looked at old Hoyt and squeezed his hand. I told him how thrilled I was to meet him and his wonderful family. I told him I'd pray for him and hoped he would get home soon. With all his might, he gently squeezed my hand. I still vividly remember the moment.

Back at the Hawkins' home, we had a blast. Hylton's mom invited Nashville's finest citizens and had them come over for a repeat of the films. The home was lovely and filled with delicious food and candies. Hylton and I went outside and smoked a big one and headed back in. Before we put the films on again, we said there were two rules while watching. "Play loud and have fun!"

Hoyt made it out of the hospital, but later died in his home of an apparent heart attack.

Hoyt was one of the founders of the Jordanaires and sang baritone. I didn't know it at the time, but the Jordanaires also sang backup for artists like Frank Sinatra, Perry Como, Tennessee Ernie Ford, and Dean Martin. The Jordanaires were regulars on the Grand Ole Opry for over 30 years.

It was my honor to have spent time with Hoyt.

Chapter 21

Duran Duran Is NOT On Our Hot Stack!

I bought a bottle of wine, poured a glass, and waited for the dreaded weekly call. It was a late July day in 1982. The phone rang and you could smell it. It was the smell of the rumpdog and he didn't waste time telling us how he felt about us.

"Job security is getting airplay!!!

"I'm disturbed!!!

"Our #1 priority, Missing Persons, is BULLSHIT!

"You've given away the store with free Beatles records and we only got 30% of the country!!!! It's #47 with a bullet in *Billboard* and we only got 10 adds on 'Words!' That is SHIT!!! It's burning out!!! We're halfway across the river!!! Are we gonna make it all the way across??? YOU TELL ME!!! YOU BETTER GET TOUGH!! I'm done bailing everyone out!!!! I'm tired of paddling by myself!!!!! It's BULLSHIT!!!

"We're #50 with a bullet on April Wine! What are we doing? Giving up? You've totally ignored this fucking smash hit!!

"Duran Duran is NOT on our hot stack! Is it a fuckin' hit or not? People tell me the band is talked about, but what the fuck!!! Do we have the right track? Try to get 'Hungry Like The Wolf' tested somewhere so it won't get in the way of what I'm trying to do here!!!!

"Okay, the new Juice Newton is 'Break It To Me Gently' and it's out Wednesday. It's the second single and I want you to treat it like a new Beatles record!!! I want a major blitz!!! Juice takes a second seat to nobody INCLUDING our own family of artists!!! She's the #1 female artist out there today. She's ALL HITS! ALL IN A ROW!! I want you to run this up the ass of your key major stations!!! Every gun blazing!!! BANG BANG BANG!!!!! PUT THIS FUCKIN' RECORD AWAY!!!!"

Chapter 22

Atlanta In Tears – August 29, 1982

It was August and time for me to head to Atlanta. Now I know how it got the name "Hotlanta!"

I had to meet up with our local guy, Gino. He was an old timer who had a big Afro haircut and drove a 70's red Cadillac convertible. I always had a hard time getting him to call me back, so I thought a visit was in order.

We got to know each other throughout the day, visiting radios stations and having lunch together. Gino introduced me to a radio guy who was a big Beatle fan and once we started talking, we were off to the races. Little did I know Gino was a big Beatle fan and collector! We had never connected on that level before.

As the day was winding down, Gino asked me if I'd like to come over to his house and have dinner with he and his wife. I was flabbergasted.

After a great meal and absolutely wonderful company, Gino invited me to the basement to see some Beatle things I might not have seen before.

As we headed down the steps, his wife yelled, "Don't forget, you guys have a conference call in 20 minutes." After Gino pulled out some Beatle trinkets and we got talking, it was time for the call. Gino told me to sit at a desk across from him and he'd put the call on the speaker.

I put my feet up on his desk and closed my eyes to listen to this week's game plan.

As the phone rang, I could smell it. It was the rumpdog and he was raring to growl. He already had his mind on a long weekend in Palm Springs. I guess his date stood him up. He was in no mood.

The call began.

"The holiday is coming and I need to put all of you in line!!!

"Before I get started, I got a note to read from Steve Miller. He says thanks for the #1 on 'Abracadabra.' He says to his knowledge, it was the first Capitol #1 since 'My Sharona' by the Knack.

"But that note is from Steve, NOT ME!

"I am pissed at this overpriced, do-nothing team!!!!

"Juice Newton is the one I wanna zero in on!!!! We got a total of 98 adds with 20 new ones last week. THAT SUCKS! Juice is an automatic, but you're letting this one just get by!!!!

"I'm disappointed in this staff! Country radio delivered!! Adult contemporary delivered!! But we didn't!!! Right now there is an awful Oliva-Newton

John, a terrible Sheena Easton and a piece of shit Kim Carnes!!!! THIS IS BULLSHIT!!!!

"Every one of you is waiting for radio to add all this shit and then you think Juice will fall in!!!

"You got us fourth in fuckin' line while those broads get ahead of us!!!!

"You're a wise ass if you're sitting back waiting for it to happen on its own!!!

"Tell those fuckin' radio people I don't care if it's too country or the second track from the album!!!! I don't fuckin' care!!!

"Shit! These other broads have had five in a row midchart records!!! They get all the attention the minute they put a record out!!!

"FUCK!!!!

"Gino!!!"

My eyes jerk open. Now he's talking to the guy sitting across from me.

"Gino! Z93, the top 40 in Atlanta, what the fuck is going on down there???????

"You working or sleeping!!!!!!

"Juice has always performed at that station and now she's the only one of these broads that AIN'T ON!!!!!

"FUCK!!!!!!!!!!

"We played all the games for that program director!!! It's BULLSHIT!!!!!

"We took him to dinner!!!! We played the bullshit Gold record game!!!!! We had Juice CALL HIM!!!!!

We had her send all the cute notes to the fuckin' guy!!!"

I open my eyes and see Gino, a grown man, crying. His head has hit the desk and there is no chance for recovery. The boss won't let up.

"You're not kicking the shit out of this guy!!!!

"It's a joke!!!!!!

"The whole staff has done a so-so job on a superstar!!!!!!"

At this point, I quietly headed upstairs and asked his wife to call me a cab to take me back to the hotel. I realized I'd better step up helping my new friend Gino with his rock airplay while he focused on his top 40 priorities. The poor guy.

While I waited for the cab, the call continued.

"Okay, remember the most important career at the label is the Motels!!! It's the hottest act in the business!!! You gotta cement 'Only The Lonely.' Screw it in and nail it tight with a fast hit and blow it out quick!!!!!

"I just know we're gonna get killed on this Labor Day weekend!!!! I know I can't count on this team!!!!

"FUCK!!!!!

"On the 'Hungry Like the Wolf' single by Duran Duran, we're getting the record played in the Boston area. It's off to a decent start. Let's see where else we can push it. Someone said it's on in Buffalo but I don't know how it's doing there. Tell the programmers it's the Police meets the Flock Of Seagulls.

"Now!!!! Let's get serious! Here's what we decided to do with Missing Persons. I said we would never stop talking about them until they are stars!!! I'm going to spend a LOT of money on this record!!! I'm gonna put independent promotion people on it!!!!! I'm gonna set it up in advance!! I'm gonna service it through the trades! I'll be doing a major blitz advertising campaign EVERYWHERE!! September 15 is the blitz date! I want an all-out CRUSH!!!! I want 40 to 50 adds!!! I want TONNAGE!! I want to show an all-out commitment!!! This is our strongest act!!! This will be a national blitz!!! This campaign will have everyone running at the same time for results!! I wanna spend money!!!! I wanna crack this group!!!

"In closing, I am in a panic over all our records!!!!!!!!! We're in for a real rough time!!! Staffs are being chopped!!! Heads are rolling all over the place!!!!! The business is very tight!!!

"I only dwell on money when it comes to HITS!!!!

"DON'T FORGET YOU HEARD THIS FROM ME….. KILL OR BE KILLED!!!!

"Have a good holiday. You're all great. I mean it!"

Chapter 23

"TOP OF THE WORLD, MA!"

Halfway through a hot summer day my brother called me and asked me to go to the Yankee game. Ed said his buddy got a limo for the evening and they had an extra ticket. They told me to be downstairs at 5:00 p.m. Since everyone had to be up early the next day, the plan was to stick around for seven innings and take a slow ride home to New Jersey. Maybe stop for a quick drink, but all in all, it would be an early evening.

So they thought.

My brother was a school teacher, so he got out at 3:00 p.m. and was half in the bag when they picked me up a few hours later. He always told me the three best things about being a teacher are July, August and 3:00 p.m. The other guys were lit up and laughing, happy to be in a huge limo, getting wrecked safely.

The seats were great and the game was fun. We spent more time drinking and telling jokes then concentrating on who was pitching or batting.

The game was close so we stuck around to see how things turned out. The Yankees lost.

Traffic around the stadium was insane so we popped into one of the bars near Yankee Stadium. It was so old we could believe their claim that Babe Ruth drank there. Seeing the old fashioned urinals, Ed-boy reasoned The Babe had probably pissed there too.

Finally it was time to leave. We flagged the driver and told him to head home. I leaned over to put on the radio and I noticed it was almost midnight. WNEW FM was playing the Beatles and my friend Danny was on the air. I suggested we head over to pick him up and have a little nightcap. He told me to meet him downstairs at the radio station around 12:20 a.m.

Around 12:30 a.m., Danny came out of the building with someone. The door opened and they both plopped in. I introduced the gang and Danny introduced his friend. It was a girl and she looked shy and just nodded her head for a few moments. We were pretty wacked at this point, so anything out of the normal would really tweak us.

Danny's friend opened her mouth to ask us where we were from, but when she spoke, she squeaked! Her voice sounded like Olive Oyl from the old Popeye cartoons or Betty Boop! We started to crack up. She was throwing one-liners at us that had us kneeling over in laughter.

We found a cool bar and fell inside laughing. Danny's chum was off the chart. She was a true original with a wicked sense of humor. She told us she was just starting out and that she was in a band called Blue Angel. She said her name was Cindy.

It was now close to 2 a.m. and these guys really had to get up for work, but nobody was going home yet. Cindy knew we were heading to the downtown Holland Tunnel, so she asked us to drop her off at CBGB's, the punk club in the Bowery. So off we went.

Hilly Krystal, the owner, was standing outside when we pulled up. We dropped the window and asked him if we could come in. He said, "Sure! The next show is about to begin!"

The gang could not believe it. A concert about to begin at 2 a.m. was something out of the twilight zone. They couldn't resist. I asked Hilly if the bar was still open and he said, "Yup, and plenty of cold beer!"

We all got in the club on a free pass from Hilly and then I looked at my brother, the teacher who was due in school in a few hours. He was at the bar with two cold, tall beer bottles with the biggest smile I'd ever seen on him. He looked at me and screamed, "TOP OF THE WORLD, MA!"

That girl Cindy? She left the band Blue Angel and struck out on her own.

She was Cyndi Lauper.

Chapter 24

Plasmatics in Poughkeepsie

Poughkeepsie, New York was the first show on the tour, which started in November of '82. The Plasmatics were now on Capitol Records and we were ready to launch their new album, "Coup d'Etat." The Plasmatics were truly groundbreaking in their approach, blending punk rock and heavy metal. Many bands would follow their lead – but in 1982, recording in Germany with Scorpions producer Dieter Dierks was a shocking choice for a punk band.

The Plasmatics were nuts. They blew up cars, destroyed televisions, were arrested for indecent exposure, and the beat goes on and on. Wendy O. Williams was the outrageous lead singer and performance artist that fueled the wild sound and sight show. The *Los Angeles Times* said, "Williams makes Ann Wilson or Pat Benatar sound like Judy Collins."

I decided to bring my young nephew to the show with me. He was 14 and had the day off. It was a long ride to Poughkeepsie and I could use the company. I told him to kick back and hang on for a long day and night.

I drove over to the venue to pick up Wendy and take her over to the rock station that was presenting the concert. Little did I know she'd be topless with black tape on her nipples. I could sense my nephew's bewilderment. I hadn't told him what band we were going to meet.

The Plasmatics had just shot a promotional film in the blazing hot desert for a song called "The Damned." The guy on the air loved the band, the album and the new song, so he asked her about the video.

Wendy said, "I drove a school bus full of explosives through a wall of televisions sets and then emerged on the roof top singing and jumping off before the bus went through another set of televisions and blew everything sky high!!!"

She said, "You asked for hell and you got it! Our new album is called "Coup d'Etat," and this is the first show on the tour."

The DJ dropped the needle and the phones lit up with Wendy's Poughkeepsie fans.

She told everyone she busted up her ankle jumping off that bus but was ready to perform this evening. The DJ asked her where someone like her goes to unwind. We were all surprised when she uttered, "Disneyland." She also said five hours after each show she wakes up and goes jogging. She told the listeners she then works out at the hotel gym if she's on the road. The interview really revealed a different side to Wendy.

Before we left, the DJ asked Wendy to cut an ID for the station. She nailed it in one take. It went like this.

"This is Wendy O. from the Plasmatics and if you don't listen to WPDH in Poughkeepsie I'm gonna come over there and I'm gonna smash your radio and tie you up and put clothespins on your nipples and whip you with a garden hose!!!"

At the gig that night they performed "Living Dead" which started with "One two, fuck you!" It's also on the record, check it out!

After the show, a few of us hit the Palace Diner in Poughkeepsie. A sign in the window said, "College ID, free glass of beer." That should have been a tip off that things could get a little wild. The joint did have a jukebox so, while everyone ordered, I checked it out. It wasn't playing but it was lit up and the bartender said it worked well.

I noticed some of the drunken college kids were throwing their weight around with the band members. It was time to get the band out.

While the shit stirring was being hurled our way, I slid over to the jukebox and saw John Lennon's "Cold Turkey." I tossed in five bucks and played the b-side over and over. It was Yoko's "Don't Worry

Kyoko (Mummy's Only Looking for Her Hand in the Snow)."

We were headed out the door when the violent wail of Yoko's screeching voice overcame the diner. Just as the door was shutting, I could hear people yelling at the bartender to turn that shit off. It was late and this bar man didn't know where the volume switch was.

We got our point across.

I thought Wendy was an incredible artist. She was like a well-built professional wrestler. She seemed to be in control, in shape, and had the means to make her art come to fruition. I saw a very bright future.

In 1998, she died after shooting herself with a gun. It was her third suicide attempt. She was 48 years old.

Chapter 25

"Hungry Like The Wolf"

The first Duran Duran album didn't sell and had no hits. We put out "Hungry Like The Wolf" – from "Rio," their second album – in June of '82, but it didn't get the attention we needed. Once we got the video to MTV, they put the damn thing in heavy rotation and the sales of the album began to grow.

By November, we had a game plan!

Ray, the head of rock promotion, got us all together for a conference call. He was talking in all capital letters!

"Gang! We got full page ads in the trades this week to declare our commitment to finally breaking Duran Duran and 'Hungry Like The Wolf.' We've picked up 16 rock stations in the past two weeks including Los Angeles, Dallas, Seattle, Atlanta, Memphis, Tampa, Syracuse, and Tulsa!

"Programmers have felt the effect of months of incredible MTV exposure. Radio is NOW ready to crusade Duran Duran.

"The changing tastes of programmers, due to the recent success of Modern Rock groups like Flock Of Seagulls and Missing Persons, has made it possible for Duran Duran to be seriously considered for rock airplay.

"When we serviced the first album nobody could hear it!!

"Meanwhile, the 'Rio' album has sold 600,000 copies worldwide, going Platinum in the U.K. and Platinum plus in Australia. 'Hungry Like The Wolf' has been top 5 in the U.K.!

"Let rock radio know that we're re-releasing that track as a single here featuring the David Kershenbaum remix.

"You should have sufficient copies of the remixed and remastered version of 'Rio' to service to all your rock stations immediately.

"The 'Rio' album has been on the *Billboard* chart for six months and is currently 1/3 up the chart. Let's go for the other 2/3's!"

On their first promo trip to New York City, the band members shared rooms at the Parker Meridien with each other. They were gracious and charming at each station visit. When we were done making our rounds, I took Duran Duran over to Parachute, an avant-garde clothing shop on Wooster Street. After the guys filled their arms with clothing, the manager came over to me and said 'Sir, the men's clothes are upstairs. This is the woman's floor.' I told the guys and they dropped everything to head upstairs. After one minute, they said 'These STINK! We like the other clothes.' So down they went and I watched my AMEX soar to over 2K.

Things broke big for Duran Duran. We took "Hungry Like The Wolf" to No. 1 on *Billboard's* Top Rock Tracks chart. The song spent 23 weeks on the *Billboard* Hot 100, peaking at No. 3, and setting the stage for a long string of hits.

By 1984, we had new guidelines to handle the backstage fiasco. In fact, it was so important, Ray demanded a conference call with the promotion team.

"Simon, John, Nick, Andy and Roger are eager to spend a few minutes meeting our key radio and retail account people, particularly important program directors. However, our precious few minutes before shows are being wasted by the attendance of 'FANS' at the receptions, who mob the band for autographs and pictures. By 'FANS' I include the children of our guests! It seems that if a fan is a child, sibling, baby-sitter or whatever to one of our guests, that fan will go any length to get into the reception!

"Coca-Cola, the sponsor of the tour, have been the worst offenders and are henceforth going to be eliminated from our receptions.

"This means that it's entirely our responsibility to make these brief meetings WORK, not just as strokes to our guests, but as an opportunity for Duran Duran to feel they've accomplished something. They want a chance to make a good impression on radio, to show that they're intelligent, mature and grateful for the support they have received.

"A bunch of kids will totally thwart this reception and burn out the band with regards to continuing with the backstage meet and greets.

"Our goal is to provide some personal contact between Duran Duran and our important radio and retail guests, in lieu of local interviews and other potential visibility, for which there is simply no time. Let's protect our investment and allow the band some quality time to make a good and lasting impression.

"Also, I can get you autographs sent from the road, so please give me your requests as opposed to allowing our receptions to turn into autograph parties.

"Remember! Except for contest winners, kids at receptions will NOT BE ALLOWED!!!!!"

By their third tour, each band member had their own suite and brought along friends like Madonna and Andy Warhol. At a party, I approached Andy Taylor and said, 'Andy, Scott Muni from WNEW wants to say hello. Come on over."

Andy said, "TELL HIM TO COME TO ME!"

Chapter 26

"I Can Make It Rain Money!"
April 22, 1983

The top 40 team was killing it with eight songs in the top 100. We had "She Blinded Me With Science" by Thomas Dolby, "Hungry Like The Wolf" by Duran Duran and "Even Now" by Bob Seger – all in the top 20. We had "Rio" by Duran Duran, "She's A Beauty" by the Tubes, "Shame On The Moon" by Bob Seger, "When I'm With You" by Sheriff, and "Walking In L.A." by Missing Persons all rounding out the Hot 100.

Yet the rumpdog was ready to crush us with another conference call. It was Friday, thereby ensuring that our weekend of mental recovery would be shattered while the boss headed to Palm Springs in his Rolls Royce to chill.

"One of our top guys is leaving! He wants to run his own ship and make a lot of money!! With that in mind, let me say, there are possibilities of other changes if we don't start working harder!!!!

"The new crunch release is Sheriff!! It's been out a long time, but now I'm spending money on it!! I was looking at it a month ago. Now, three to four weeks later we have movement. The buzz is there. I'm getting feedback that the record is performing so I am making it our #1 priority!!! I mentioned it to the independents and they told me they had it on the radio four months ago.

I told them, 'SO WHAT! GET IT ON AGAIN!!!'

"People are scratching their heads! There IS confusion!! They're wondering!! But if I show a commitment attached with MONEY we can bring it home!!!! I am convinced this is a fuckin' hit record!!

"Here's the stack of acts and records YOU BETTER BREAK!! Red Rider, Amy Holland, Nielsen/Pearson and Maze!!! Maze is the hottest new R&B record out there!!!

"This may be a crossover!!! I wanna break it if it's breakable!!! You got to BATTLE!!!!! I'm gonna pay the independents!!!! We gotta sell albums!!!

"Last year was a rough year but I can see the wheel turning. My goal is to blow out records! I got money to spiff the independents!!!! I can make it RAIN MONEY!!!! I can give out raises!!

"It's rough but NOTHING WILL STOP ME!!!!!!"

Chapter 27

Spinal Tap

H elix was a band on Capitol that flirted the airwaves with "Heavy Metal Love" and "Rock You"
from the albums called, "No Rest for the Wicked"
and "Walkin' the Razor's Edge." The core of the
band was a trio of guys from Canada. They were a
fun gang that didn't take themselves too seriously,
and tried hard to find that big hook that would score
them success in the U.S.

They did a cover version of "Gimme Gimme
Good Lovin,'" originally by a band who called themselves Crazy Elephant. It was almost a top 10 hit in
America. Helix did it with a twist. They used topless
models in the video to create a Miss Rock Fantasy.
Among the girls in the video was 16-year-old porn
actress Tracy Lords.

The guys were begging for attention.

The band and I got along great and one day they
arrived at our offices in New York City. Instead of

going to lunch, I asked the guys if they'd like to see a movie in the middle of the afternoon. I told them a little about the movie "This Is Spinal Tap" and they were interested. I was lucky since the movie was playing right down the block from the office.

Ten minutes into the movie, which is about a band on the road, I was laughing uncontrollably. I looked over and the fellas were stone faced. They were serious.

A few minutes later my laughing fit came back, but they were still watching it like it was a real documentary.

There's a scene where the band leaves the dressing room and heads to the stage, but they get lost trying to find their way. It was funny, but the lead singer sitting next to me wasn't laughing. He cried out, "That really happened to us!" He said it in such a direct way that I laughed even harder. Everything that happened in the movie seemed to have happened to these guys, which made me bust a gut.

We made our way back to the office and word got out we spent the afternoon at the movies.

Later in the day, the President of the company stopped by the office. He was here from California and, of course, he runs into the Helix guys and he asks them what's been going on. "Dave took us to the movie this afternoon!" I could see it didn't make sense to him so I told him about Spinal Tap the best I could. After 10 or 15 minutes, he let it go, but I could tell he wasn't happy I was at the movies in the middle of the day.

The President flew off to England for the weekend and I went home to chill in the suburbs.

On Monday, Rod Smallwood, Iron Maiden's manager, was in the office. I looked at him with a devilish smile. I told him, of all people, he had to see Spinal Tap right now. Do not pass go, do not collect $200. We have to go immediately.

Rod was up for it. We had an hour to kill so, as Rod would say, "Let's hit the pub, mate!" We drank a few and got caught up with all things Maiden. Rod was the genius when it came to the success of the group. They even changed lead singers and it was no big deal. It was a theatrical show with great heavy metal songs.

The movie began and Rod lost it before I did. He's a big man, like Chas Chandler of the Animals. Immediately Rod was laughing so hard he fell off his seat. I had to get my arms around him to get him back up. The both of us were falling apart laughing. We had a buzz on before we arrived and now we were both beet red. He was laughing at the screen and I was laughing at him laughing at the movie. We really fell apart in the theatre.

The movie ended and, believe it or not, we saw the actor who plays the drummer who dies onstage of spontaneous human combustion. We went over to shake his hand. He couldn't believe he was recognized so we invited him out for a liquid lunch. We laughed for another hour and then Rod and I headed up to the Capitol building.

We had laughed so hard and drank so much we actually fell out of the elevator and into the lobby. The label President was standing there, just looking at us. He could tell we were wasted and it wasn't even four o'clock in the afternoon. I tried to get real sober real fast, but I'm no magician.

It was good being with Rod since his sales on Iron Maiden meant so much to the company. We sat down to talk and Rod wouldn't stop going on and on about Spinal Tap. The president had no idea what we were talking about. I did my very best to communicate to him that seeing was believing, but he wasn't buying it.

About six months later, I was able to buy a copy of the movie. The first thing I did was call the President and tell him the movie was on the way to the Tower. He didn't sound like he was interested. Still, I hoped he would give it a chance. If he fell on the floor laughing too, I just might redeem myself.

A week went by and, out of the blue, the President of Capitol called me.

"Morrell, I took that video home with me not knowing what the hell the damn thing was about. After dinner on Saturday, I told my wife and son to come in the living room. I wanted to see what they thought of it too.

I was dying on the other end of the phone. I couldn't believe he'd show his wife. The President was much older than me and I thought she must be old too – and not likely to get this kind of humor.

"I put in on and in the first 10 minutes my wife didn't understand what was going on," he said.

"Ha," I said with a whimper. I could feel the crushing defeat coming.

"She left the room so I watched it with my son," he said.

"How old is he?" I asked.

"He's an older teenager. I figured he might like it too, but after a half hour he didn't want to watch it anymore."

I could feel the knife in my heart. I was feeling like a loser thinking I took this damn thing too far. What the hell was I thinking?

The President continued, "I could see they weren't into it so after they left, I closed the door and put it on louder. I started laughing my ass off. It was terrific! My wife came in and wondered what was wrong with me. She said I was cackling! Morrell, that movie was great and I'm glad you took all those guys to see it! I plan on doing the same thing. Great job!"

Chapter 28

Iron Maiden At Shea Stadium

Prior to the 1984 World Slavery Tour beginning in Poland, Rod, the manager of Iron Maiden, called me. He said he was in town with the Maiden boys and they wanted to go to a baseball game in New York. He asked me to come along. I told him I could make a few calls and get us some great seats but he balked. He said the guys weren't like that. He said they were simple guys who would be happy just to go. He wondered if it would be sold out and I told him no. "Let's just get tickets for the game when we arrive," he said.

We loaded up the car and starting heading out of the city towards Queens where Shea Stadium was located. The Yankees were away at the time so we went to see the Mets. On the way over, Rod sat in the front while I did the driving. Rod lit up a cigarette, took a drag, and began to tell me about his new signing. A band called W.A.S.P.

He said the letters stood for We Are Sex Perverts. He said it with a straight face. I looked at him like he was crazy. Then he told me their first release was called, "Animal (Fuck Like a Beast)." I knew he was fucking with me. But he wasn't. He said there would be black t-shirts with the word W.A.S.P. on the front and the words "I Fuck Like a Beast" on the back. He said everyone would want one. I was starting to giggle. I thought this was wilder than Spinal Tap!

He said the lead singer was called Blackie Lawless and he wore riding chaps that exposed his ass. I was barely able to drive, I was laughing so hard. He said the guitar player was a guy who liked to growl named Chris Holmes who they called Chewbacca, after the Star Wars character. He said Chris was almost 7 feet tall and had come from a band called Slave.

It was all I could take before arriving at Shea for the ballgame.

When we arrived, we just walked over to the ticket booth and bought the tickets like regular fans would. We walked in and sat in the outfield down the third base side. Right before game time, a few fans saw the band and yelled, "Hey, it's Iron Maiden!" But the other kids balked and said, "They wouldn't be sitting in these shit seats, they must be imposters." We giggled. The band loved the non-attention. They band were just a group of quiet guys. Steve, the bass player, and Dave, the guitar player, were the nicest guys in the world. Steve loved going record hunting. These guys didn't do hard drugs and stay up all night. They drank beer and loved sports and the Beatles.

The Mets didn't sell out the game, but I'm sure a date with Iron Maiden would have done the trick.

Last I heard of Blackie Lawless, he was selling his Malibu home for millions of dollars.

Who'd a thunk?

Smart management! Smart guy!

Chapter 29

Enter Mr. Cattle Prod

In March of 1984, Mr. Hollywood left Capitol and Walter Lee took over the promotion department. Walter had had a long, illustrious career with the company up to that point. He had done promotion and sales in his time. He was well respected and a good choice to run the team. He was almost the opposite of Mr. Hollywood. He was a married man with kids. There was nothing fancy about Walter. He liked me, I liked him and we got along great. He put his foot on the top 40 staff and called the rock guys "the wine and cheese party planners!"

When Walter took over the staff of 22 promotion people, his old buddy from down south in Dallas thought it would be a riot to send him a three-foot-long cattle prod. He told Walter he may need to use it on a few people to keep them in line. Ha-ha, what a joke.

From that moment on, Walter proudly became the guy everyone called Mr. Cattle Prod.

As Walter was taking control of the team, there was talk out of the Capitol Tower that he was poking people and threatening people to make them jump. Some of the stories said he never stunned anybody and it was all a joke. I was 3,000 miles away so I didn't care what was going on.

I didn't have a clue.

Chapter 30

Bob Seger Turns The Page

My career as a promotion man began back in '74 at Warner Bros. Records. I worked the singles in the New York City market. I was 21 years old.

In August, while the rest of the country was focused on Tricky Dicky aka President Richard Nixon resigning, I was focused on getting airplay with a new tune creeping up on *Billboard*. It was sitting back at 80 on the Top 100 charts but it was #1 in our office. It was called "Get Out Of Denver" and it was by Bob Seger.

When the needle hit the wax, the track took off like a rocket ship. It was movin' so fast people found it impossible to hear the words. Once it bit you, it never let go. At the end of a hard day, we'd play it real loud and everything else would cease! You'd crouch down in a duck walk and with attitude you'd blow out the words as fast a Bob was spitting them out! We wore the vinyl out!

"Get Out Of Denver" was a turntable hit. Radio didn't embrace it.

By December of 1974, the old famous Fillmore East, which closed in 1971, was re-opening as the New Fillmore East. The first show featured Bob Seger opening for Bachman, Turner, Overdrive. I was excited but I couldn't get anyone to go. New York was buzzing with excitement from the recent Thanksgiving performance of John Lennon performing at Elton John's show and the upcoming final tour shows of George Harrison. Even my boss didn't want to go that far downtown. He said, "You need an Army tank to get me below 14th Street!"

Warner Bros. tried and tried again to score a hit for Bob but nothing would stick at the slick top 40 format.

The following year, Bob signed to Capitol Records and released "Beautiful Loser," then put out a monster album, "Live Bullet," followed by the classic "Night Moves."

Bob, with Capitol, went on to score huge hits like "Mainstreet," "Rock and Roll Never Forgets," "Still the Same," "Hollywood Nights," "We've Got Tonight," and, closing out the 70's, "Old Time Rock and Roll."

It was 1980 when I caught up to Bob again. I joined Capitol and to my wonderment I got to work his new smash album "Against The Wind." It included iconic songs like "Fire Lake," "Against the Wind," "You'll

Accomp'ny Me," "The Horizontal Bop," and "Her Strut," which is my all-time favorite juke box record.

With Seger, I could do nothing as a promotion man but stay on top of the airplay. Bob was a superstar before I got there. He had a well-oiled machine. He knew the Capitol promotion staff better than I did. In New York, he already had top relationships, almost friendships, with the key FM DJs. I just held on to the tail end of the comet, watched his shows and had a ball with him and the band backstage.

He sold out Madison Square Garden four consecutive nights. The reviews of the New York shows, from the most jaded critics in the world, were terrific!

Backstage at one of the shows, I told Bob about going to see him open the New Fillmore East after it closed under Bill Graham's watch back in the old Warner Bros. days. He laughed and said, "Yeah, I remember that gig too. I never got paid!"

Chapter 31

The Aftershow

The Bob Seger tour played a weekend date in Providence, RI so the NY Sales Manager and I flew into Boston to catch a ride with the local Boston representative, Tony. Besides working together, we all liked each other. Sometimes Tony would stay at my home if he was going to attend a NY Sales Meeting. Everything was smooth as can be. We drove to Providence, parked the car, and picked up our nightly backstage passes. Tony had radio guests on the list, too.

The show was magnificent. Seger was on fire! We loved every minute of the performance. The NY Sales Manager and I had seen the show at least five times already. It was a Saturday night and the good vibes were all around. Nobody had to get up in the morning.

After the show, Bob graciously met and hung out with the group we assembled. It was perfect!

Tony, the Sales Manager and I headed back to Boston to continue our little shindig. Tony kept telling us the Combat Zone in Boston is a blast after 2 a.m. on a weekend. We couldn't wait to get there. On the way out of the concert we grabbed a few beers to drink. Tony had some great weed rolled and we even had something to powder our noses with.

It was about 1:30 a.m. when the car started to choke on the highway. Tony ran out of gas. We could see a ramp up ahead and Tony figured there would be a gas station there. The sales guy got out of the car and walked to the front between the headlights and took a leak. Tony and I scoured the trunk, looking for something to put the gas in. He had nothing so he settled for an empty beer bottle that was rolling around on the floor. In the dark of the night, Tony was out of sight.

The sales guy and I hopped back in and did a little blow. Within a nanosecond, we saw the police lights coming toward us.

"SHIT!!!!" I yelled.

"FUCK!!!" the sales guy screamed.

The cop got out and was headed towards us. He asked us out of the car. We obliged.

We told him we ran out of gas and our friend went up ahead to try to find some.

As the policeman was listening to our story, we could see Tony running toward us.

"I got the gas!!!" he said happily.

"Is that an open bottle of beer in your hand?" the cop asked.

"No, sir! It's the gas for the car!"

"It's against the law to have gasoline in an open container! Where did you get that gas?"

"Right up the ramp! I gave the guy a twenty to fill it up."

Tony began to open the gas tank and fill it with the beer bottle. It would be enough to get the car to the station.

"You fellas get moving! I'm going to visit the gas station but before I go, I noticed water underneath the front of your car. Looks like the radiator might need a look-see. Make sure you have it checked."

There was the policeman, standing in the piss, watching to see what Tony was gonna do with the empty beer bottle. Tony tossed it in the trunk and off we went.

The cop car pulled out ahead of us with the red lights on and headed up the ramp. We followed, hoping to fill the car with gas, but as we pulled in, the gas attendant has his arms flailing. He was angry and started to yell at us to get out of there.

We ended up at another station further up the road. By now our big Combat Zone party plans were looking slim but Tony said to cheer up. He had the coke dealer waiting for us in Beantown.

I'd met the dealer before with Tony. He was a real odd ball. I'll call him Jumper, but that wasn't his name. Jumper's big thing was to call his home on a speaker box and play his messages back. He played a tape of a man who sounded insane. The guy on the tape was begging him for blow. Screaming for blow. Crying for blow. It was unreal and sad. Jumper told us the voice on the tape belonged to Steven Tyler of Aerosmith. It was wild! I'll never know if the voice really belonged to Tyler, but the message was one I'll never forget. It made me vow never to get to that dark place.

Chapter 32

Yoko Ono

I was 19 and she was 39 when we first met. John was 32 years old and working with a band over at Record Plant East, the recording studio. Howard Smith, who wrote the Scenes column in the *Village Voice* newspaper and had a radio show, called me up and said John wanted to meet me.

When Howard and I arrived at the studio, John Lennon greeted us at the entrance door. He ushered us into a tiny studio and asked us to sit down while he finished a session. He was working with David Peel and the Lower East Side. I didn't like what I was hearing. I thought they were wasting his time. Peel and his boys were dummies who mumbled and couldn't keep in tune. They were working on an album called "The Pope Smokes Dope."

I didn't notice at the time, but Yoko wasn't in the studio.

The Peel session took a break and John was ready to shoot the shit. I had a suitcase full of Beatle trinkets I thought he might like to see. In his recent interview with Howard, he said he had a soft spot for the Beatles so I thought this would be a perfect time. One of the items I took out was a Beatle bubblegum card showing what the Beatles would look like if they were bald. It was silly and I wondered what John would think of it so I showed it to him. "I look Japanese," he yelled while grinning ear to ear. "You've got to show this to Yoko," he said to me. John told me she was outside in the hall on a chair, reading a book. I said, "Excuse me, Yoko, John wanted me to show this to you, he thought it was funny." She was wearing a black turtleneck and looked up at me as though I was disturbing her. She took the card from my hand. Without a word, she took a pen out and signed her name on it and then looked up at me and said, "Here." She handed the card back to me and that was it. I was kinda stunned, thinking I had no story to tell John when I went back in. Good thing he didn't ask me.

The years rolled by and, after I joined Capitol, I had many opportunities to work with her.

In January of '86, Yoko Ono and Capitol Records (and a few other sponsors) cordially invited the press, radio and retail to the library and museum of the Performing Arts at Lincoln Center for the premiere of "John Lennon Live In New York City."

Yoko was stunning that evening. She brought Julian and Sean with her. Being the promotion man with a list of guests, I was grateful to bring the three of them around to meet everyone.

The evening was a celebration of John & Yoko's performance many years earlier, and since I had witnessed the shows, it brought back many memories.

The summer of 1972 had been wonderful. In June, I saw Elvis Presley play his first ever New York City full concert. In July, The Rolling Stones came to the Garden with Stevie Wonder opening. There were three shows and I saw them all.

In August, John Lennon performed! TWICE! The Madison Square Garden "One To One" concerts were to benefit the children at Willowbrook State School, a Staten Island facility for the mentally challenged where conditions were deplorable. Reporter Geraldo Rivera had brought the issue to John and Yoko's attention. My friend and I got tickets for both shows. John's headline performances would mark the only rehearsed and full-length concerts of his solo career.

The first show was like a rehearsal since John stopped a song and started over. By the evening performance, he was on fire. He ended the show with a ferocious, blazing version of "Hound Dog," before launching into the encore of "Give Peace A Chance."

Back at Lincoln Center, more than a decade later, we all settled in to watch a filmed performance of those historic shows. There is so little footage of John Lennon performing live, the film moved the audience to a standing ovation. At Capitol, we prepared a 12" digitally remastered version of "Imagine," backed with "Come Together," to take to radio stations.

After the Lincoln Center shindig, I took Yoko over to do the nationally respected syndicated radio interview show "Rockline."

The guys putting the show together had a simple but challenging request. "Rockline" had built up stations across the country to carry their shows and went out of their way to capitalize on any artist that was in the studio. In this case, they asked Yoko if she would do an ID for the stations that carried the show. Since the show wasn't run on WNEW FM in New York, there was no way I was going to let Yoko do an ID for a station that didn't support her and John since the very beginning. Scott Muni, the WNEW Program Director, would have been livid if he heard his competition had Yoko's support. When the guy tried to strong arm me, I told him to show me the whole list. I sliced a ton of stations off that were in my markets. Yoko took me aside and thanked me.

The next time Yoko and I met was over the "Menlove Avenue" album Capitol was putting out. By the way, when I first found out about the album, Capitol was calling it "Manlove Avenue" instead of "Menlove Avenue," the street where John was brought up by his Aunt Mimi. I called the head of marketing and told him they had the wrong street.

I also told him I had been to John's home in Woolton, outside of Liverpool, and had some great color photos of the house they could use for the cover of the album.

Capitol corrected the title but ended up not using my pictures. When I asked for them back, he said he couldn't find them. I never got them back.

Weeks later, Helen, from the Dakota, called and said Yoko needed a box of "Menlove Avenue" albums. She asked me if I would messenger them over. I told her I was headed over that way and could drop them off. She said she didn't want to trouble me.

The concierge's office gave me the okay to head over to Studio One and I started my journey. I was flabbergasted by how beautiful the building was. It wasn't worn down. The brass was shining. It was a masterpiece.

When I went into Studio One, where John & Yoko had an office, I was surprised how big the room was. It was all white and full of file cabinets. Some so high you needed a ladder.

I was sitting in Studio One talking to Helen when Yoko came through the door. She was very quiet and spoke softly.

She asked me if I'd like a cup of tea and I said yes. We began to talk and then she took a phone call. When she got off, she asked me if I'd like another cup of tea. I said yes. We talked a few more minutes and then she had to take another call. When she finished, she asked me if I'd like some more tea. I said yes. I was hoping to get down to business before another cup of tea arrived.

Finally, she said to me, "David, I've worked very hard on the "Menlove" project and it's been time consuming. I have yet to see anything in *Billboard* or *Rolling Stone*. Do you know when ads and reviews will be running?"

I said, "May I use your phone? I'll call the Tower and bring you instantly up to date."

"Yes," she said and handed me the phone.

She stood over me while I was sitting and the phone was ringing on the other end.

Ray, my current boss, picked up the phone and asked me where I was.

"I'm at the Dakota with Yoko!"

"Morrell at the Dakota, you lucky guy! What's up?"

"Ray, Yoko hasn't seen anything on "Menlove Avenue" in the press. What's the deal with *Billboard* and *Rolling Stone*? What's the deal with the reviews?"

"Dave, is she there with you now?" he said giggling.

"Yes, standing right here."

"Shit Dave, let me think." There was a pause. "I got an idea to save you. Ask her for her fax number."

I asked her and I repeated it to Ray.

"Dave, tell her we'll fax the info pronto, would that be okay?"

I told her and she said yes that would be fine.

Then Ray said to me, "Dave, this isn't a work record. This is simply a catalog item. We're not spending a dime on it. There are no ads. It wasn't sent out for reviews."

I was turning beat red. Ray was laughing in my ear. I was losing it.

I said, "Yoko, the fax will be arriving shortly, I gotta get back, Thank you for the tea." I practically ran out of there.

Just a few weeks later, in a sudden burst of activity, my boss Ray asked me to get together with Yoko to discuss a special limited-edition white vinyl Christmas card 12" record of "Happy Xmas (War Is Over)." When you called the Dakota, the phone would be picked up by either Helen or George. I arranged a meeting with Yoko and got my facts together.

We drank tea and got to work. It was easy and fun with no rough patches.

Back at the Tower, Ray sent the staff a note that read:

"Kudos to Dave Morrell who got together with Yoko Ono to create our 'official-approved, limited edition' John & Yoko Christmas card 12-inch of 'Happy Xmas (War Is Over).' Don't underestimate the collectability of these records. Be sure that they don't get lost among the regular releases. They should be given special attention! Make sure they reach your key people! Once the word is out, you'll be hit on by collectors, and since this is valuable by virtue of being a limited pressing, there will be no more!"

To my great joy, a few weeks later during the holiday season, I received a Christmas card from Yoko. I was moved.

To my great surprise, it was the first of many Christmas cards from her and Sean, and sometimes signed by her close friend Sam (Havadtoy).

Chapter 33

Rolling Stone Magazine

In April of '81, Ringo graced the cover of *Rolling Stone* magazine. Brant Mewborn interviewed him and it became the cover story. For Brant, it was a very big deal. He loved the Beatles and was now at Ringo's home asking him anything he wanted. A Beatle and a cover story and now Brant was turning his attention on a very special Beatles 20th anniversary special to commemorate their 1964 arrival in America. It was so special *Rolling Stone* put it out with two different covers. It was the first time they did that. It was coming in February of '84 and Brant made it well known to all his peers he wanted to be involved in some capacity.

Brant and I met but where and when remains cloudy. We used to hang out at Il Pescatore Veneto, a small restaurant on 56th Street. One day Brant had an idea for the *Rolling Stone* Beatles issue. He said, "Dave, let's do it on the collectors of rare tapes. It's a side that I love and find interesting. Will you help me?" "Of course," I said, "I'd be honored."

After a few days, we hooked up again. I had a handful of names and numbers of guys I knew who had some wonderful unreleased Beatle tracks. One of the guys sold bootlegs down in the Village. Brant was excited at the prospect. I also gave him the name of a kid who knew about different mixes, longer endings and unreleased songs. Brant was really excited to meet this guy too. I wished him good luck and went about my merry way.

The following week, Brant came up the office and was grim. He said none of the contacts called him back and those that did wouldn't speak to him. He told me he was committed to the story and *Rolling Stone* bosses were expecting a good piece of work since Brant worked so hard to be part of the special Beatles issue.

I picked up the phone and put it on the speaker so Brant could join me. I called the guy downtown with the record store and he freaked out. Before I could even speak he went on a rant about constantly being busted by the cops and his inventory confiscated. He wanted to operate below the radar and didn't want *Rolling Stone* telling the world his name and address. I could see his point.

The guy with the rare tapes barked too. And he bit. He was furious and didn't even want to be on the phone with a writer from *Rolling Stone* magazine. I was aghast. I felt I let Brant down. The guy said if anyone knew what he had, Apple would be over there getting it all back. This guy did not want to be featured in a Beatles *Rolling Stone* issue and told me if I co-operated I would be out of my mind.

Finally – with no interviews completed and his deadline rapidly approaching – Brant asked if he could interview me and show some of my Beatles tape collection. I told him I had to really think this over. After all, I worked at Capitol Records and someone might think something fishy was going on. I called my boss and asked him if he thought it would be okay.

At the 11th hour, Capitol brass gave me the go-ahead to do the interview with Brant. He sent a photographer over to the house to take a picture of a trunk stuffed with rare records and reel-to-reel tapes. It was a treasure chest for sure.

He wanted to call the story "I'd Love To Turn You On" but settled for "Beyond Beatlemania." The subhead read: "Studio outtakes, rare concert tapes – Dave Morrell knows how to find the Beatles music that the world wasn't supposed to hear."

Capitol Records had executives who sat on the prestigious EMI International Beatles Committee which was originally founded in response to Beatle bootlegs. Brant called Capitol A&R Manager, John Carter, who was so much fun, he wrote "Incense and

Peppermint" by the Strawberry Alarm Clock. Brant wondered why a guy like me wasn't part of the conversation regarding the Beatles.

Carter said, "As far as I'm concerned, Dave knows ten times as much as anyone on the committee and I hope he can help us with future projects. "Right now, we're trying to drop the tacky repackages we've been so criticized for in the past. Dave's boss seems to think The Motels and Iron Maiden need more of his attention. Most of the committee are just plain folks, not Beatle experts."

I had hoped the article would generate mail from other Beatles collectors, thereby expanding our database of historic materials and facilitating the exchange of information between fans. My radio appearances with Howard Smith had always brought a lot of mail, but the *Rolling Stone* story only elicited two letters to the editor. Published in the following issue, they were not positive. Still, I was pleased that Brant had so eloquently captured the role collectors play in preserving precious pieces of history.

Brant and I became fast friends and the future was bright. He continued to write and went on to form a band with his girlfriend Rhonda. Eventually they married and invited me to their wedding. They threw a terrific party on a boat in the Hudson river for their friends – a group that included Sylvia Miles, the actress from *Midnight Cowboy*.

Brant and Rhonda got a place upstate and he invited me to visit, I never made it up there. I didn't realize Brant was ill.

He died of AIDS at the age of 39.

I'm still heartbroken. Brant was a bright light who loved life and the Beatles.

Chapter 34

Albert Goldman's On The Phone!

The receptionist got a hold of me and asked if I'd take a call from Albert Goldman regarding John Lennon. This was odd. He wrote a book about Elvis that I read and thought was a low blow to the King. I picked up the phone and introduced myself. He spoke like a businessman, not a music guy, and said he was doing a book on John Lennon. He said he had cooperation from many of John's close associates who wanted to speak openly. I told him I didn't like what he did to Elvis and he told me that Elvis hid behind closed doors and had a private life no one knew about. I was starting to yawn. He told me things were different with John. He said everyone knew about John's private life. That John hung himself naked outside to show the world his true self. He said John was James Dean, a true hero, icon, and a guy who wore his heart on his sleeve.

By now he had my attention. He said he wanted to write the greatest book ever on John and I believed him. I told him we should meet and he agreed. He lived at Columbus Circle, on 59th Street where you enter Central Park. It was an old building and he had a good view. He looked like Ben Franklin does on the 100 dollar bill but spoke with a high shrill voice. I asked him what he was looking for and he told me he just needed simple sales and release dates of John's work. Easy for me to get. He also said he needed anything I could find on Yoko's early work before she met John. Mostly newspaper clippings about her far-out work. He also showed me some things he had gotten that nobody knew about. Now I was hungry to see and hear what he was talking about.

He opened a safe and out came the treasure trove. There were tapes and letters. He told me one of John's employees took John's personal diaries for two reasons. He said John's wish was for Julian, John's son, to have them and that if Yoko kept them, she would read them and take out the bad stuff about her.

I saw six weeks worth of John's writing that he did alone in Japan. When he felt he was done, he sent the paperwork to himself at the Dakota. On the envelope John wrote, "It's to me from me, don't open!" In one entry he writes about his Aunt Mimi reading his work when he was younger and breaking his sex code entries, "the witch!" he wrote! He then writes about Yoko coming into the room and wondering whether he should continue to write and let her see it or stop and keep it quiet. While reading this private material, I could understand the points Albert was making. In another entry John goes into detail about his "secret prayer." He also talks about his writing and how bad he felt it was over the past few years. John's notes on his visit, which included his accounts of the weather, also match up with later accounts written by John's tarot card reader John Green, who wrote a book around this time frame. There were also reports from John's publicist, who was going to meet him at the time. John mentions these encounters from his side, so the documents are real and authentic. Goldman also pulled out tapes of John that no one had heard before. "Grow Old With Me" on acoustic guitar was incredible. Most of the demos out there are with John on piano. I felt Goldman was really on to things and he was moving forward rapidly.

I put my thinking cap on and got to work immediately. It turns out I had a souvenir program from Yoko's show in Syracuse, NY. The program folded out like a big newspaper and inside of it were news clippings of her early work in New York City. This was too good to be true.

I met with Albert on several occasions. He was coming up with so many twists and turns, my head was spinning. I knew I had to share this experience with someone else. I called up my Beatle buddy who was a writer for *The New York Times*. I figured as history passed, he could back up what went down at Albert's joint.

Albert's book came out and he stabbed all of John's friends in the back. Yoko was pissed and stopped speaking to many of her friends. The world was pissed. My buddy, representing *The New York Times*, interviewed Albert about the book. After confronting him on many subjects, Albert became defensive, even denying having previously met my friend.

Chapter 35

Manhattan Records - June 27, 1985

Manhattan Records was presenting a new band produced by Ian Hunter and Mick Ronson. They were a New York band called Urgent. "Running Back" was the first single from the album "Cast The First Stone." It was a big priority for Manhattan, and the staff at Capitol would be promoting it, so we had a call with the head of Manhattan Records.

"Everybody get their Urgent albums in yet?" he asked.

"Yeah," one of the guys replied.

"What? There's only one guy on the call? Everybody feel pretty positive with this record???" he barked.

"Yeah, it's a good song," someone said.

"It's the best thing we got coming down the pike. I don't think I've heard a new act with a stronger album than this in a long time!!" the Manhattan guy told us.

All of a sudden Mr. Cattle Prod decided to take over the phone call.

"We'll get back to Manhattan in a moment, but first, I've got a few things I want to mention.

"There is a press announcement that went to the trades this week. I wanna talk about the staff restructuring that's gone on the last couple of days. We have restructured our rock division. Bill Bartlett remains national director. Bill will have two associates. Dave Morrell in New York and Stan Gleason, who will move to the Tower.

"The Heart record, 'What About Love,' must be closed out! It's the #1 Priority. We've brought them back from the dead! We absolutely must do it! The initial outlay of the Heart album is 300,000 units!!! Pretty impressive! We must take this single top 10. It's a deep album and if we can catch a second or third single, we'll sell millions, but we must score that first single.

"Freddie Jackson. We picked up the big top 40 in Los Angeles! We gotta fight for big chart jumps! We are close to 400,000 albums!! It was #1 on the R&B chart for six weeks!! The longest #1 in Capitol's history on the R&B chart and we're going for week seven!!!

"Tina Turner's 'We Don't Need Another Hero' had 147 adds the first week! That makes it the most added!! We need another 40 adds to break it wide open! The reaction to the record is great. MTV is whacking the video and the movie, "Mad Max Beyond Thunderdome," opens July 12. We've got everything going for us on this record. Let's make sure we take this record top 5 and we have a shot at a #1 record.

"Duran Duran. We went 3* to 2* with 'A View To A Kill.' Need I say more!!!! We don't stop at two!! The sales department is all geared up to go for it next week. We gotta keep radio up there as high as we can. Get as many #1 reports as you can and let's take it to #1. A point I wanna bring up with the side project of Andy and John's Power Station. The guys are getting a lot of hate mail from the fans accusing Andy and John of splitting up Duran Duran. John and Andy will be appearing with Duran Duran at Live Aid and as soon as the Power Station tour is over, they will rejoin Duran Duran in Europe to work on the next Duran Duran album. These guys are too smart to leave a money-making operation like Duran Duran.

"Alright, let's get into the Manhattan Records."

The Manhattan Records guy took over the call again.

"The World Sitizenz are out there with a new album and the single we're working is 'Lock It Up.' We've been out there playing with these small focaccia Gavin radio stations and we got enough this week. I think we got 23 reports out of 38 stations and we are now in the 'additional records' category. I think the important thing for you to do, beyond the visits and the calls you're making to radio stations, is go for the low hanging fruit. The small stations. I know this record is a real struggle for you out there and we're up against the wall with any new act when it comes to top 40 radio, but we're gonna stay with this thing and build a momentum slowly but surely. I'm not asking you to blow in 40 to 50 top 40 stations, but I do want you to get me these little focaccia stations. Go after the little stations!!! Now, the last time we talked we said everyone would bring in one station and everybody said they could get somebody. Nobody came up with one!!! That's not a one-week deal!! I hope you guys are still out there committed to getting me that station you told me you would!! I know you're working on them. If you need help, I'm here to help you get them. We want to do what is necessary to get this record off the ground! It's time for us to see momentum on this record. If we do get a few adds next week, we'll have to work it even harder! Make a point to call the small stations and point this out to them.

The head of Manhattan Records promotion said, "We started the call talking about Urgent's 'Cast The First Stone' before Walter took over. Let's get back to it. There are a couple of real basic things that have to be done. Make sure those radio people are listening to this record. I know they get a lot of records, but make them listen to this thing and DON'T ASK THEM IF THEY LIKE IT OR NOT!!!! TELL THEM

THAT THIS IS A GREAT RECORD! We know it's a great record, we're behind it. We believe in it. This is full tilt boogie. You're going to get a lot of screaming and yelling from me on this record. It's a mainstream record and it's in the pocket for you. I know you guys can do it! It's time for Manhattan Records to get on the map here! That's it for me. Walter, please take over again."

Walter took back the telephone.

"We have yet to show Manhattan Records what we're capable of doing. They're sitting on the side-lines watching Katrina & the Waves go flying through here and Heart over there and now Freddie Jackson and they're sure anxious to get their turn in the barrel.

We covered a handful of other acts, then he closed out the call.

"Before we go, you can plan on another conference call in two weeks! I was thinking of having one next week but I want to go work on my tan.

"So let's get the buzz going on the Motels, let's see what the hell we can get going on Manhattan Records by showing some style, take care of Heart, bring home Helix, a big week on Katrina & the Waves, let's get something going on Luba, take care of the rock format, do it all, let's go out there and be the #1 team for Capitol and Manhattan!"

Chapter 36

Payola, Circa 1986

I t was a couple of days after my birthday and I was laying low for the weekend. It was on Monday, February 24, 1986 when things turned for the worse.

The buzz on the street was NBC TV was going to run a report about payola in the music business later in the evening.

Since I was on the East Coast, I'd get to see it before the folks at the Tower in L.A. I stayed away from the office that day and made phone calls from home. Later I headed over to my mother's house to have dinner.

We turned on the TV set and began to watch.

Within the first 10 seconds, they ran a film clip of Mr. Cattle Prod with an independent radio promoter, who the anchorman identified as an alleged mobster with ties to organized crime. While we regional promotion people always grumbled about the indies and the big bucks they were paid compared to us, this news was a shocker!

I wanted to hide under the bed.

My mother said, "That's your boss??????????"

The headlines screamed, "Alleged involvement with organized crime!" "Leadership of industry was knowledgeable and involved!!!" "People won't come forward due to threats of being physically hurt."

The report said a number of record labels had been subpoenaed including CBS, RCA, Capitol and MCA!! It said the independent promotion people were changing their names and being hired for staff promotion jobs!!!

I poured another glass of wine and knew this story wasn't going to go down well at the Tower.

I imagined Mr. Cattle Prod's days were numbered.

Chapter 37

Mr. Cattle Prod Zapping The Phone Lines!

Sales were soaring!

It was early June of 1986 and Capitol Records was flying high! Bob Seger's "Like A Rock" was at three million albums and he was about to go out and tour for nine months. The self-titled Heart album was heading to Quintuple Platinum and their first #1 album. It included "What About Love," "Never," their #1 song "These Dreams," and now we were working a fourth single, "Nothin' At All." Plans were made for a fifth single from the album called "If Looks Could Kill." We had just released a new Joe Cocker album called "Cocker" which included "Shelter Me" that we were working at top 40. Crowded House was brand new and tons of money was being thrown around to come out of the box strong with big radio market adds. There were big expectations for the group. Meanwhile we were just given the new single from

Queen called "A Kind Of Magic" from the album of the same name. It would go on to sell six million albums worldwide. It was their first album since their dynamic Live Aid performance. We hadn't scored a hit for them yet.

When you add up the sales of those records and the number of singles we were scoring from albums, you could see we were grinning ear to ear. It was a marvelous time to be working at Capitol Records except when the phone rang and it was another conference call to make us feel ill.

I could smell the call coming. It was the rump-dog. His cattle prod was hissing on the other end of the horn.

"Okay, let's get started!" he shouted.

"Bob Seger's 'Like A Rock' is a goddamn embarrassment! The airplay activity on the single absolutely must catch up to the sales reporting activity! The chart jump must improve! We gotta go top 10!! Simple as that! Look at every station in your market and if the song didn't jump 3 or 4 points you better get your ass in gear!! You better be consulting with your salesmen to figure out a plan! It's your responsibility! For the rock album stations let's start working the song 'Aftermath.' We have a new extended version which you'll be getting in a few weeks. Start working it now!

"On the Heart single, 'Nothin' At All,' we have to get this single top 5! There will be another single from the album, but we have not scheduled it 'cause we're gonna take this record top 5. Right now, we're at #12 in *Billboard*. Next week the record is either going to #9 or #10. In fact, it better go to #9. Once we get the record top 10 in *Billboard*, then we'll take it top 5, then we'll set up the next single, 'If Looks Could Kill.'

"Okay, we got that out of the way, now let's discuss a hit record with Joe Cocker. 'Shelter Me' is a great record and we've done a terrible job! Awful! I'm sick over it! You've got to go back and focus at all formats and make people believe! We're over a half a million units sold….in EUROPE!! If he can sell a half a million over there, imagine what we can do here! You're sleeping, folks! Get out and get the job done! You've done a lousy job on the Cocker record. He's out there on a promo tour so let's use him!

"Hey Cleveland! How'd everything go with Cocker when you took him around town?" Mr. Cattle prod prodded."

"Perfect!" the promotion man chimed in. "Joe's got a great personality. People really like him and he's a good talker!"

"Good," said Mr. Cattle Prod. "Hey Detroit, tell us how it went."

"Absolutely fabulous," the Detroit guy chirped into the phone.

"Chicago! What happened with Joe in your town?" the boss man asked.

The Chicago guy yelled, "He won everybody over! He's going into the monthly sales meeting to present his own album!!!"

Mr. Cattle Prod thought about that for a moment and said, "So...Cocker's going into a monthly sales meeting and present his own album. You know what? He's gonna dazzle everyone! We gotta break this record. It's a great record and Cocker's a great guy! Let's make sure it gets done!"

"Now let's get into the Crowded House project. I can't believe the complete lack of activity!!! I am stunned!!! Their lead guy was in Split Enz and every one of their records on A&M sold 350,000 consistently! Take that to the bank!! With the new signing to Capitol Records and all the hoopla, the bullshit, the teaser ads, tip sheet coverage, the talk and the buzz, what do we get? Bubkus!!! I was talking to a tipsheet guy and he talked to 20 radio stations and they all said, 'Haven't heard the record!!!!' That was yesterday. A week after we serviced the record and people are saying they haven't heard the record? What do you do? Drop it off at the front door? Make them listen to this fuckin' record!!!! This is a great record, I think. Maybe it isn't. Once thing for sure, a lot of people haven't heard it. I've heard it! I've got an opinion! People can't have an opinion until they hear the record!! So next week I want you to go to every rock station in your market. You make them listen to the record and, after listening, it's your job to talk them into adding 'Don't Dream It's Over'!!! Next week I want two rock adds from everyone and guess what? If you get them, I'll send you $150.00! That's it!!!

"Hey Boston, you think you can get two adds on Crowded House next week?"

"Sure!" the guy piped up.

Then he asked the guy in Chicago. "Hey Chicago? What about you?"

No answer came back. He asked again. "Hey Chicago? What about you?"

Still no answer so the Rumdog barked "Earth to Chicago! Chicago, you with us?"

"Fuck him! Let's move on. I'll fry his ass later!" he scowled.

"Now I wanna talk about the Queen record! 'A Kind Of Magic' from the album of the same name. A lot of you don't have the impression we are serious about the group!!! They are HUGE in the UK and all over the world. The album is already #2 in the UK. Now I'm here to tell you this isn't just another Queen record!!! Here's the plan. All of you will have a copy of the video! It's a fabulous video, one of the best videos we've ever made! It premieres on MTV tomorrow night!!! Now get this. Queen asked us to offer radio stations trips to the UK plus one of YOU gets to go too!!! Queen is a fuckin' hit record! It's the first Queen record that going to be hit! It's a hit! We MUST DELIVER on this record! We MUST have a big first week! Let's come out of the shoot and have a monster week!! If we come out with four adds, forget it!!!!! It's over!!!!! We ain't gonna get it!!! We must do it!! You have to use all of your energy to get people to listen to it!! I don't wanna hear people haven't heard it!!! How do you promote records if you can't get people to listen to it!!! That's where your first creative thought process has to go! How do I get them to listen? The Queen record is being inserted in all the tip sheets so everyone will get it! *Billboard* is servicing it to 350 top 40 stations!! They'll have full color page ads! Everyone will have the record but that doesn't guarantee everyone will hear it!! You've got to get the message across! If nothing else, YOU must listen to the Queen record!!! If we have 50 to 60 top 40 adds, the entire industry will stand up and take notice!!!"

He hung up and we all got to work.

Chapter 38

Capitol Punishment

I t had been a stifling hot day in New York City. The New Music Seminar was in town and the folks at Capitol rented a Staten Island ferry for the evening. It looked good on the invitation and now that the day was done it was time to hit a few bars, down a couple of cold ones and ship ahoy!

Capitol asked Paul Shaffer to be the Captain of the evening and he hardily agreed, even wearing a captain's sailor hat for the voyage. The whole idea was to fill the boat with tastemakers, managers, salesmen, club DJs, and radio people. Everyone with a New Music Seminar badge was welcome to board the ferry.

We'd float off lower Manhattan and then the boat would dock and we'd be welcomed by one of our new bands performing. We had Skinny Puppy, East of Eden, Grapes of Wrath, Reivers, and Fetchin' Bones.

I got on the boat with Rod Smallwood, Iron Maiden's manager, and we headed directly to the bar. Inside the ship, it was boiling hot. There was no air conditioning and nobody opened the windows. We knew we had to grab the beers and head on deck where we could catch a breeze while watching Manhattan disappear in the background. Rod figured we needed at least a six-pack to take with us. The bartender told him they didn't have time to chill the beer and they only got 10 cases for the cruise. Rod was livid and demanded six beers. We got them and headed up the stairs. Once we got to the back of the ship we could see the boat was still filling up. We thought we'd get a hundred people but we were looking at a thousand.

We popped the beer and it exploded out of the can. We lost half of it. The other half was hot. Hot beer on a hot night was not on our list of things to do. We decided we had to get out off the boat. We got downstairs and walked through the closed cabin, which was like being locked in a container with no air and too many people. The bar scene was completely unruly. With all our effort, we still couldn't make our way out of the ship and on to dry land.

The boat took off and headed to Staten Island. The trip takes 30 minutes. We were fucked. We think one of the bands played on the ship, but there was no way we could get to them. We were soaking from the humidity and getting grouchy. We put our thinking caps on and figured as soon as we got to Staten Island we could grab a cab back to the city.

The boat didn't dock so we couldn't get off. Everyone was pissed and cursing and gasping for air. The band Skinny Puppy was playing live and everyone was yelling at the same time. Nobody was in the mood for their sound.

The New Music Seminar was supposed to be a gathering of new artists hoping to be signed, but this year it was all hype and hoopla to get people out to see the bands signed on Capitol.

Our launch was the worst and the bands went down in history as being part of the "Capitol Punishment" boat ride to hell.

The following year the New Music Seminar left the Big Apple and headed to Austin, Texas, never to return.

Chapter 39

Paul McCartney

P aul is back!
   That's all I needed to hear.

Capitol re-signed Paul and we were rushing out his new single, "Spies Like Us," from the film of the same name. To get a title song in a movie was a huge deal. Just think of "Live and Let Die," from the James Bond series. I couldn't have dreamed of a better launch for Paul. It was November of 1985. The stars of the movie were from the famous "Saturday Night Live" TV cast. They included Chevy Chase and Dan Aykroyd (one of the original Blues Brothers). Everything about the launch seemed perfect.

It wasn't.

Capitol had a screening of the movie before it was released. We invited everyone. You could feel the excitement when the lights went down. Once the movie started, things seemed off. The movie didn't open with Paul's song. By the time the movie was concluding we still hadn't heard Paul's new song. It was baffling. Finally the credits started to roll and they played the END of Paul's track. It was terrible. It wasn't even a song. After the end of the song was played first, they played the whole track, but by this time the theatre was empty. This wasn't a good sign or even a stat we could take to radio to try to get it played.

I was such a big fan of Paul's but this song just didn't move me. I've heard it a thousand times, but the melody still to this day doesn't stick in my head.

At Capitol, we dug deep and used all our resources to make sure we came out strong and delivered for Paul. When all was said and done, we were able to take it top 10. It peaked in *Billboard* at 7*. Paul wouldn't have another top 10 single until "Four, Five, Seconds," over 30 years later.

In July 1985, Capitol ramped up promotion for Paul's newest effort, "Press," from his new album "Press to Play." The big news this time? Paul is coming to New York to promote it. You know what that means? I get to work with him. Pinch me! I must be dreaming!

Hearing about the album set my heart beating fast. Pete Townsend from the Who was on it. Phil Collins from Genesis was on it. My expectations were running wild.

George Hurrell, the glamour photographer who took pictures back in the day of Clark Gable and

Greta Garbo, took the cover photo of Paul & Linda using the same box camera he used in his famous Hollywood days. It was a striking cover that people could use as a talking point while playing the music on the air.

Paul and Capitol launched "Press to Play" with a big party in the lobby of the famous Radio City Music Hall. Tables were set up and Paul requested we have a CD player chock full of goodies. He himself brought Little Richard's Greatest Hits to play.

I didn't have much of a relationship with the very top dogs at the company and they were all there. Bhaskar Menon, the worldwide head of the company, was there with the President of Capitol in the United States, Don Zimmermann. I stood making small talk with these guys when Paul made his entrance. I could feel people moving to the front of the lobby and I could see flashbulbs going off that were blinding my eyesight. Everyone was caught off guard when Paul entered from another direction. When my eyes came back into focus, there he was, standing right next to me. It happened so quickly.

Paul quickly shook hands with Bhaskar and then with Don and then he looked at me like he wanted to shake my hand. Don jumped in and told Paul that I was Dave and that I was the album promotion guy based in New York. He told Paul I was a big Beatle fan, too! Paul shook my hand and said, "Hey man, good to meet you, what's one of your favorite songs on the album?"

Without skipping a beat I hopped right in. I was thinking of the song "Move Over Busker" from the new album, but I got tongue-tied with the Chairman of the board, Bhaskar, standing on the other side of me so I said to Paul, "My favorite song that I'm telling the DJ's about is 'Move Over BHASKAR.'"

There was silence. Then Bhaskar looked bewildered as if Paul had written a song with the word Bhaskar in it. Paul started to giggle and that turned into a full laugh as he said to me, "You mean 'Move Over Busker?'" It was then I caught myself and felt foolish, but Paul punched me on the shoulder and said he could understand how that popped out of my mouth.

I told him the New York radio folks would love to meet him and have their picture taken with him. He said no problem and we both strolled around the room. Everybody got his or her turn and nobody pushed or shoved. Paul took his time and answered every question asked of him. When we finished, the press person took him around to meet all the other guests.

While this was going on, I went over to introduce myself to Linda, Paul's wife. She was with Danny Fields, who was a writer and personal friends of hers. I knew Danny was there covering the story for a trade paper. Danny had worked at *16 Magazine* when the

Beatle craze was at its zaniest. Linda asked to no one in particular if they had anything to smoke? I told her I did. She said to Danny and I, "Let's get lost," and we did. We were like kids looking to hide so we ran upstairs and inside the Radio City Music Hall Theater. It was massive and empty and gorgeous.

After we lit up and got quiet while inhaling, Linda leaned forward and asked me if I'd ever seen a motion picture here at Radio City. I was thrilled and delighted to say, "Yes, it was a movie called 'The Yellow Rolls Royce.'" She stopped, looked me directly in the eye and said, "That was crap." I wasn't sure if I was going to choke or laugh. "That was a crummy movie, did you like it?" she said. "I did," I replied. "I was a kid and I liked cars." She laughed and then told us she saw "Show Boat" here with her high school mates. She remembered dancing down the aisle when it was over.

I had my Polaroid camera with me and asked her if I could take a few photos of her. She said sure. She kept one for a souvenir. I had been so extremely excited to meet Paul, I had to bring the Polaroid. I needed instant gratification. I couldn't wait the week or so for the professional pictures to come back.

After a good long smoke and small talk, we made our way back downstairs. By now people were beginning to sit down and enjoy themselves. As we made our way towards Paul, Linda took me by the arm. I figured I'd go sit with the Capitol gang, but Paul saw us and began to laugh. He said, "You two have the munch-ies! I can tell! You're sitting with me!" The next thing I know I'm sitting with Paul and Linda having a meal.

The first thing out of Paul's mouth was to me. He said, "What's going on at Capitol?" I was stoned and off guard but that didn't stop me from saying, "All of us are so happy to finally see a rare Beatles session record coming out officially!"

"It's rubbish," he said. "It isn't coming out." I was taken aback and told him it was already in the Capitol Records sales catalog and the salesmen were taking orders.

"What's on it?" he asked me. I told him some early takes of songs like "I Am the Walrus," for instance.

He said, "Who picked those? Who decided what earlier takes were the one to go with?"

I said I didn't know.

"The final versions are the ones worth hearing. Those are the ones that are exactly how we wanted them to be. Don't waste your time on the few takes before," he said.

I moved his attention on to another point. I asked, "What about songs the Beatles wrote for others?"

"Like what?" he responded.

"'Come & Get It.' Your demo of it sounds great! Exactly like the way Badfinger did it."

"That's right. I told the boys to do it just like the demo I made. That's the hit record!"

"You were right! It sure sounds terrific." I babbled.

Then I said, "What about original songs the Beatles did that never came out?"

"Name one," he said.

"I thought for a moment and then said, "How 'bout 'That Means a Lot?'"

At this moment, he took his left hand and put it up to his throat using to fingers to pinch his Adams apple and than began to sing.

"Can't you seeeeeee, can't you seeeeee, rubbish," he said laughing. "I'd never want anyone to hear that mess."

The whole table was laughing by now.

Lunch came and went and Paul and Linda both wished Capitol had just served pizza. People began leaving. I retrieved Paul's Little Richard CD and handed it back to him. Paul said I could have it. I've still got it.

I took out the rare John Lennon Beatle Butcher cover that John had given to me and I asked Paul if he would please sign it for me. He took the album in his hands and stared at it. He saw John's autograph to me and said, "If John's signature wasn't on here, I'd nick this off ya! I haven't seen one of these in years!" So with a smile and a good luck nod, he placed his signature on it. It was an unbelievable moment for me. It was like making it to the top of Mount Everest!

I'd be seeing and working with Paul again.

Capitol pushed and shoved its way up the charts with the "Press to Play" album. We released it in

August and it made it to #30 on the *Billboard* chart. The following week, it went backwards to #36 and had lost the bullet that shows strong upward movement. "Press to Play" went down as the lowest charting album of his solo career, apart from the official interview album from 1980 called "McCartney Interview" on CBS Records, which was deleted from their catalog the same day it was released.

The single "Press" made it to #25.

It got tougher. "Stranglehold" was the next single from the album and it debuted at #97. That was the lowest number for a single Paul ever had except for "Hi Hi Hi" which came on the chart at #100, but finally made its way to the top 10. On the other hand, "Stranglehold" peaked at #81. In other words, it was a bomb. We kept going and chased another single, "Only Love Remains," but that one didn't chart at all.

The follow up came a year later. It was called "Flowers in the Dirt." The album would come out first, followed by an American tour. Now I'd get to not only work with Paul's record, but I'd get to go to the shows and bring people back to meet him. I was wild with excitement.

From "Flowers in the Dirt," the first single was "My Brave Face" which came out in May of '89, followed by the album in June, and then the tour of America in September.

The single was strong, but only made it to #25. That kind of number on the charts kept the big New York top 40 stations from playing it.

The "Sessions" album of unreleased material never came out due to objections from the surviving Beatles. It took another ten years before they put their collective thoughts together to form the successful Beatles Anthology series.

Chapter 40

A Month Later

Mr. Cattle Prod is back at the Tower after seeing Queen in the UK. He's buzzed and pissed as he starts up the next promotion call. He starts with Queen's single "A Kind Of Magic." We've been out promoting it for the past 30 days. The expensive video is all over MTV, everyone has the record, the full color ads are everywhere. The salesmen are laying out tons of albums. The promo team has to deliver airplay at radio.

The Rumpdog started the call.

"WE'RE DOING THE FUCKIN' FOX TROT!!!!!

"We lose four radio stations and pick up six new adds!!! We get seven stations and lose five!!! WHAT THE FUCK! We need 20 stations!!!!! Three weeks ago, I was blown away. I went to Wembley to see the band. 75,000 people were all amazed. There were 150,000 folks at two shows who paid $22 a ticket! Everyone knew every song! Springsteen at the L.A. Coliseum is the only one I've seen like that. Take this message

out to the radio stations; this is the European counterpart to Springsteen. Only the Rolling Stones and
Springsteen have sold out two shows at Wembley and
that's pretty good company. Next week we hit hard
with the Queen record!! We can't allow ourselves to
be sitting here next week with 100 radio stations on
Queen!!! THIS RECORD IS TOP PRIORITY!!! ARE
WE ALL IN TUNE WITH THAT?

"Yes, sir!" everyone said in unison.

"Okay, let's move to Heart. The new single is 'If
Looks Could Kill.' WE HAVE TO HAVE A REALLY
BIG WEEK!!! All Heart has done is quietly sold 3 ½
million albums and have four top 10 singles and a #1
album!!! This record is happening!!! We HAVE TO
GET TONNAGE!! We have to sell another million
copies!! The Eagle in Dallas added it at #14 with a
HOT REPORT! Take that message forward!!! The
record is HAPPENING!!!

"Over to the new Paul McCartney, "Press To Play."
It was a good first week, so let's get this record out
of the way!!! Let's clean it up at radio! Get another
50-60 stations and let's get it done with!! We had over
100 stations the first week!! Come on! Let's get this
through the system!!! We have a McCartney album
coming the later part of August. Let's go and make
this the biggest Paul McCartney album since he left
Capitol!!! LET'S BURY CBS RECORDS!!!

"On the new Missing Persons album, 'Color In
Your Life,' we have an opportunity to re-establish

the group. We picked up 15 tiny stations this week! That's the bad news!! The good news is we got KIIS FM in Los Angeles!!! Not to0 shabby!!! KROQ in L.A. has been playing this record for a few weeks and it's selling! It's in heavy rotation and the sales have really kicked in!!!! Let's get the damn thing played!!!!

"The Beatles! This is really unique! In yesterday's marketing meeting, I pointed out that in the last 10-15 years we've always been trying to come up with some bullshit hooks to sell Beatles catalog! We'd get some records out, we'd merchandise them, we'd sell some and that would be the end of it! Well thanks to two movies (*Ferris Bueller's Day Off* and *Twist & Shout*) people are re-discovering the Beatles! The 'Twist & Shout' single you ran with last week was already added in Houston! Not too shabby!!! They added it at #16 with a HOT REPORT! KIIS FM in L.A., which added it two weeks ago, has gone from #30-#16 with a HOT REPORT!!! So, we've only got two stations playing the Beatles and both of them gave it hot reports!! The opportunities are mind-boggling!!!! If this record breaks wide open the money will be pouring in.

"We happen to have a Beatles catalog that has sold about half a billion dollars' worth of records over the past 25 years!!!!! Could it be the Beatles break all over again????? 'Twist & Shout' is on three Beatles albums. It's on 'The Early Beatles' and it's on 'Live At The Hollywood Bowl' which is a dog version! It's also on the Beatles 'Rock & Roll', which is a green line series album priced at $5.98 but in checking the other day there is no inventory on the green line series album and we probably won't manufacture anymore. Why sell it for $5.98 when we can sell it at $8.98 right?????? Order yourself 50 copies of 'The Early Beatles' albums and service your stations and tell the story!!! Let's quietly sell a couple of million Beatles albums! I guarantee the President won't be upset and neither will I!!!!!

"Okay, let me mention a SLEEPER HIT that NEEDS YOUR ATTENTION! It's Sly Fox singing 'Let's Go All The Way!!!!' It's #1 in HOUSTON!!!!!

"Ashford & Simpson have an R&B smash! What can you deliver at pop radio??? Work it!!! It's called 'Count Your Blessings.' Go listen to the damn thing!!!!

"On Wednesday, you'll be receiving the new Bob Seger single, 'It's You.' The album is still in the top 10 and we're at five million in sales!!! Seger already hit the road and the speed at which the shows are selling out are mind-boggling!!! Outside of Chicago, at Alpine, Bob did two shows. He sold 36,000 tickets quicker than Springsteen. The shows are spectacular! The crowd reaction is incredible!! I was there last night and every person, young and old, was standing and waving their hands! When Seger comes to your city, you have to make sure that the proper radio people are at the show to see that the magic is still there!!! I'm telling you RIGHT FUCKIN' NOW 'It's You' is a smash that will go right through the system!!! You're not going to accept ANY negatives on Bob Seger!!!! You can write that down on the back of your wrists!!!!

"Coming in three weeks, 'Typical Male' from Tina Turner! It's from the album 'Break Every Rule.' Wednesday, August 13 is BLITZ DAY!!!! You are to coordinate this rollout with your R&B promotion manager. I don't want a top 40 station to get this record before the black urban stations or vice-versa. Game plan is for every station to get it at the same time!"

Just when you think the call is over and you need to lay down, Mr. Cattle Prod hands the call over to the rock department. Ray was back in charge. He had gone on to his dream job signing bands for Capitol Records but now he was running the rock promotion department.

Ray began, "'Press,' by Paul McCartney, was #4 most-added at the rock stations. McCartney hasn't been a household name at rock radio for a long time. Our mission here is to kick CBS's ass and show them we can do a better job. We have the best record that McCartney's made in quite a few years for rock radio and we have the tools to do the job. We have to go for a quick closeout. There are tracks on the album the rock stations are going to love and embrace. We are going to surprise everyone and release a track that is kick ass rock & roll! Then we'll carry it to the top of the charts. It's called 'Angry' and it's Paul, Pete Townsend and Phil Collins rocking out!

"Now let me tell you about my pet project, Great White. I was involved with the band before I left A&R. I went down and saw this band. They're a spectacular live rock & roll band. They've got a lot of the qualities that people saw in Def Leopard in the early days. They have a rock & roll attitude. They are not a heavy metal band but they certainly will be able to secure part of that audience because they do kick ass. The thing with Great White is they have great songs and the guy is a great singer plus they got a great guitar player. These are all the ingredients to make a superior band. This is a crusade project. We've got the opportunity here to do what Elektra did for Dokken, what Polydor is attempting to do with Cinderella. It's basically to show a commitment to the act. We're going to take it through the fuckin' system! We're gonna stay with it and we're going to come up with a barrage of tools and ammunition to keep this thing going! This is the one we have to get in the trenches with and be very proud of! Make sure that our radio people get it! We're gonna bring it home! We picked up a dozen adds this week! The subjective reaction from radio was outstanding! Some programmers are making comparisons to early Led Zeppelin!! WE NEED TO BREAK A ROCK & ROLL BAND!!!!

"The Crowded House album has just gone out. I want everyone to ask for album reports so we can get most added! We're going to get picks and tips. The feedback I've gotten from radio says they are not sure if it's a rock album project! Inevitably they will love the album and respect it. Order some promotion cassettes and get them out to your radio peeps. Let them live with it. We are a month from releasing a single for a song that is absolute magic! It's called 'Don't Dream It's Over.' That will be a combined rock and top 40 blitz! It's one of those kinds of records we have to make a commitment to. It's a superior song! It's not a formula hit record. I want you to get your people into the album now!!!

"The Heart track, 'If Looks Could Kill,' has been making the rounds at rock radio. It is the top priority at top 40, so let's try to bring this track back!

"On Bob Seger we did a sensational job with 'Aftermath!' We've held the record up at the top 10 of the rock charts. Mention the tour! There is new life due to Bob being out on the road."

The called ended and immediately Ray rang me up.

"Dave! Book it, man! I'm sending you out here. I want you to see Great White. They're booked to do a first anniversary show for KNAC, the rock station that broke them."

I flew out and saw the band play across the street from the Capitol Tower. Great White played a sold-out headline show at the Palace Theatre and they rocked! They played the single "Face The Day" from their debut album "Shot In The Dark." In typical fashion, the backstage area was a scene! Coke, porn stars, champagne and a bunch of Capitol Records folks. I had a great time meeting the band and talking about their upcoming first visit to New York City.

A few weeks later Jack Russell, the lead singer of Great White, sent me a postcard. I was surprised because I never expected he would remember me by name.

Chapter 41

Once Bitten, Twice Shy

I was sitting on the porch when the mailman arrived. He handed me a great looking postcard from beautiful Marina del Rey, California. It was from my friend who used to be the Apple House Hippie, Richard DiLello.

"Yow! Dave! Thanks for everything! I had dinner with Derek last night and saw a copy of his book which I haven't yet purchased, but will. Things are okay here. How 'bout youz?' King Kobra - the greatest! - Again, thanks, Richard.

King Kobra was a hard rock band founded by the great Carmine Appice, a super great drummer and big Beatles fan! Considering the records I usually sent to Richard, it was a kick that he dug King Kobra. The album was called "Ready To Strike." I remember the first time I heard it: for some nutty reason, the band had flown us all to Los Angeles to party at a bowling alley and listen to the record on some really terrible sound equipment. We took it to radio but King Kobra never got the attention Capitol was looking for. Years later the lead singer Mark Free went through a sex change and became Marcie Free.

Derek was Derek Taylor, and he wrote a wonderful book called "Fifty Years Adrift," which I consider a masterpiece. He was the Beatles Press Officer, among many other achievements. Richard worked with Derek at the London headquarters of Apple Records. Derek's book was very expensive and limited but worth it. In one part, he had me laughing out loud. He was describing a moment in New York on one of the Beatle tours when a young girl grabbed Ringo's St. Christopher's medal from around his neck. Derek went to great lengths to describe the DJ's reporting on this unfortunate incident.

As my mind was racing and my stomach hurting from the laughter, I realized I had a tape of that moment in my collection of Beatles stuff, so I made a copy for him. While I was at it, I also added some rare Beatles' tapes I thought might pique his interest, and sent it to him via the book publisher. Since the books were numbered, I just signed the note with the number of my book. I figured if he liked it, he'd have to ask them who I was and perhaps where I lived. We had met numerous times before and I thought the ruse would amuse him.

A month went by and then a letter from England arrived at my home address. It was from Derek.

He said he got together with Neil Aspinall, a fifth Beatle, and head of Apple, and they both listened to the tapes. He said they laughed out loud when they heard the DJ's crying over the radio airwaves for the quick return of poor Ringo's medal, which they did manage to get back. They even brought the girl up to meet the fab one. She said she just lost all control of herself and had to have it. He wrote that Neil and he were flabbergasted at the acoustic version of George's beautiful haunting "While My Guitar Gently Weeps."

The following week I received another postcard from Marina del Rey. This time it was from my new friend Jack Russell, the lead singer of Great White.

"Yo Dave, 'The Wanderer' here is still on the go. Thought I'd drop a line and say HEY! Stay Cool. Jack Russell."

Jack was mischievous. He was like a surfer dude that didn't like rules. But I dug him, the band, and their music. It was great rock & roll. Jack sounded like Robert Plant so he had a tough time convincing people he was original. Once the band started covering Led Zeppelin songs, it was over as far as radio programmers were concerned. But at this moment in time, Jack and one of the boys were flying to New York to begin a huge promo tour. It was Sunday evening when they arrived at Newark Airport in New Jersey. I picked them up and took them to dinner, then dropped them at the hotel. I told them we had an early start Monday and we were due over at WNEW FM for lunch. I told them I'd get them at 11 a.m. Before Jack hopped out, he hit me up for 50 bucks.

"Fifty bucks for what? You just ate! It's time to go to bed!"

He looked at me like I didn't trust him and said, "Dave, it's for breakfast. We get up early and want to get off to a great start. These hotels food bills are too big for us! Help a band out, brother Dave!"

With a bit of grumbling I handed him 50 bucks and we called it a night.

I got home and went to bed. It was almost midnight.

At 3 a.m. my phone rang. I picked it up and it was Jack.

"Dave, we're in the city and we need a lift to our hotel. We have no money."

"What are you doing in the city when I told you to stay put?" I asked.

"We came to the city to buy a camera I had my eyes on," he said.

"I'm not buying it. What the fuck's going on? Use the 50 bucks I gave you and take a cab back to the hotel. I'll see you in the morning."

"Dave, I used the money to buy the camera. We're stuck here with no money and no way to get back. Please come and get us!"

"Where are you?" I asked him.

"We're on Eighth Street and Waverley Avenue."

"There are no camera shops over there. I know that corner!" I barked at him.

"Dave, we need your help. Come and get us, we have a full day ahead of us and we can't fuck it up! Please come!!"

I grab the car keys and head over. I find myself in the middle of Greenwich Village at 4 a.m. looking for these two bozos.

I see them, pull over and honk my horn for them to hop in. For some reason they both jump into the back seat. As I go to pull out, I see a third person has hopped in. It's a guy and he's smoking crack cocaine! I hit the brakes as hard as I could at 5 miles an hour and threw them all out of the car. I told Jack he was fucked. I told him the cops confiscate your car if there's any crack! They got rid of the guy and ran up the block to where I was pulled over. Jack came clean and said he actually sold his camera and, with my 50 bucks, he was able to cop some crack.

At that point, I didn't give a shit about these guys. I was exhausted and had to work. They were rock & rollers who never got tired and the party never ended.

After the Great White promotional tour, I was back in touch with the House Hippie. I continued to write letters and send him albums. He was doing great! Little did I know he wrote the official follow up to the award-winning movie "The French Connection."

"Dear Dave - Thanks for all the sounds! I wrote and produced a two-hour TV movie for 20th Century Fox & NBC called "Popeye Doyle." It will air Sunday, Sept. 7, on NBC at 9 p.m. My shirt size is extra-large if you get any great t-shirts. - Thanks again, Richard."

The following day, the mailman delivered a racy postcard from Hamburg. It came from the wonderful Beatles collector extraordinaire Charles Rosenay!!! with three exclamation points after his name. That's his thing.

"Well, I'm back in Sin City and it's still nothing but peep shows, night clubs and remnants of a quarter decade ago. Horst Fasher is hosting us here and his stories are nothing short of fantastic. Remind me to tell you the 'Lennon' story. Save me everything that comes through on 'Press to Play.' I'll call when I get back. Tomorrow it's off to London and then Liverpool! Cheers, Charles!!!"

Chapter 42

Crowded House

The staff got the album in the mail and after hearing it, everyone knew it was special. The rest of the world didn't know it yet. The promo staff delivered it to the radio stations, but if you didn't point it out of the stack and play it for the right people, they ignored it. At first it was just a question of getting people to hear it, then they would believe. Then we found out the formats we thought would be right for Crowded House didn't work out. We couldn't get college, rock or alternative stations to engage.

Finally, the bell rang. We had to follow the same plan as Elektra did with Simply Red. We had to chase "Don't Dream It's Over" at the adult contemporary radio stations.

In New York City, we did have the rock station WNEW FM on board. The staff was really into the record and wanted to break them. When Crowded House arrived in town for the very first time, they didn't even wait for their luggage at the airport. They got their gear and met me over at the station. We went directly on the air and the band blew New York away with their wonderful sense of humor, originality, and easy listening melodies that carried through the airwaves. They played songs from their self-titled debut album and engaged the listening audience with funny quips and barbs. Their immediate take on New York was funny. They were like the Marx Brothers and the Beatles rolled into one.

While on the air they mentioned a super surprise show happening at CBGB's where tickets were only five bucks. It quickly sold out. The place was hopping and going mad with fun when Crowded House hit the stage.

Backstage, before they went out for another encore, Neil Finn was saying they ran out of songs. He turned to me and said, "Dave, when we get back out there you yell 'Whole Lotta Love' by Led Zeppelin. I said, "Are you kidding?" Neil said, "We do it!

We got back out and the band took the stage. I got behind those standing and while Neil was saying they've run out of tunes and asking what we would like to hear, I yelled out at the top of my lungs, "Play 'Whole Lotta Love'!!!!!!!" Every head in the place turned to look at me, bewildered. All of a sudden, Neil broke into the guitar riff and nailed it perfectly. The place went crazy. We laughed so hard.

Finally, the show was over and the band was backstage and it was getting very late. The President at the time was the great Bruce Lundvall, who was cool and laidback and had seen it all. Bruce wanted to go home and didn't want to wait around for a new band, so he knocked on the door of Neil's room to be let in. Neil said to wait a moment, but Bruce just opened the door. There was Neil in his underwear with a tall woman – a foot taller – in full embrace. It made me crack up. I was thankful I had a job that gave me such pleasure – and involved staying up late, hearing great music and hanging out with the leaders of our industry.

Neil broke away from the gal and shook Bruce's hand. The other 99% of Bruce was already halfway out the door.

It floored me that earlier in the day it was just me and the disc jockey in the studio while these three guys called Crowded House were playing "Don't Dream It's Over" live over the air.

As the years rolled by, the song became a classic with tens of thousands of fans singing along with the band.

It saddened all of us to find out years later that the wonderful, unique and very funny drummer, Paul Hester, committed suicide.

Chapter 43

Billy Vera & Sgt. Pepper

I flew to L.A. to hang with Ray, my rock boss. The first stop of the evening was a juke joint in Santa Monica to catch the great, but not yet well known Billy Vera.

Billy wrote tunes for Fats Domino, Rick Nelson, Dolly Parton, Robert Plant, Bonnie Raitt and Elvis. Billy had produced hundreds of albums and now, in 1987, at 44 years of age, he was on the verge of having a #1 record in *Billboard*.

Man, was he in a good mood – and for good reason. Standing next to Billy was a legendary movie star. It was Angie Dickinson, TV's "Police Woman," who was called Sgt. Pepper in the television show. After doing some mental math, I smiled to myself and thought – it was (nearly) 20 years ago today that the Beatles had released an album involving another Sgt. Pepper.

Angie was dating Billy. She was 13 years older than him but looked like she was in her 20s! She had dated Johnny Carson, Frank Sinatra, Dean Martin, William Shatner and John F. Kennedy! She had even been married to Burt Bacharach.

I said hello to her and tried to introduce myself into her life, but she only had eyes for Billy, who sang his heart out to her. I was so excited, I called my mother back east where it was 3 a.m., just to tell her who I was with. She said I scared her by calling so late but she was happy for me and I could tell her all about it another time. I told her we took a picture and I'd show her as soon as I got a copy.

A guy who worked on the TV show "Family Ties" saw Billy sing an original song called "At This Moment" and got permission to use it in an episode. America went nuts when they heard the song. It hit #1 on the *Billboard* Hot 100 in January 1987 – six years after it was first released as a single.

Chapter 44

Liverpool

I made the mad mistake of going to Liverpool in cold November with only thin socks and my Beatle boots. What a nut job!

I jumped a train in London and headed north. I thought it would be an easy, cheap trip and boy, was I wrong. The ticket to the Beatles mecca emptied my wallet and the journey seemed to take forever.

When I got to Lime Street Station, I wanted to wander around the train station. It was so old! It opened in 1836 and is the oldest mainline station in the whole world. But I was pressed for time and had to make a fast break for a bank.

A flip of the coin at the exit would tell me to head left or right for the bank.

I walked right and came upon a bank and walked in. The one guy behind the counter had long hair so I thought I was in good hands.

He asked me where I was heading and I told him my first stop was going to be John Lennon's childhood home. The guy stopped what he was doing and glared at me. Then, with an evil stare, he corrected me, "John Lennon didn't live in Liverpool! He lived in Woolton!!"

I was stunned. The only other person who worked at the bank began to approach me. He seemed very old and was hunched over. I thought he may not have a kind word either but he gently asked me if I liked the Beatles.

I told him I was a big fan from America.

He told me to wait a moment.

He came around the cage and said he was a fan, too!

He wrestled around in his wallet and pulled out his membership card to the Cavern Club where the Beatles really got going! He told me he got off for lunch in a half an hour and asked if I would like to see the sights with him. I smiled.

We hopped in his car and chugged off. I'll bet we didn't get three blocks when he yelled, "LOOK! It's Queenie!"

"Who's that?" I asked.

"That's Brian Epstein's MUM!!" he proudly replied.

"I missed her! Can we go around the block?"

By the time we made our way back around, she was gone. My new buddy thought she might have gone into the meat shop for some sausage and wondered if I wanted to wait for her to come out.

Back on the road, he drove over to John's home on Menlove Avenue.

It was much nicer than I ever imagined. John was brought up in a beautiful little cottage with stained glass on a nice block of homes. I took a few photos and we left but we didn't have to go far. Right around the block is where John would ride his bike. It was called Strawberry Fields.

It was fab! It was probably the highlight of my trip.

The next stop was Penny Lane and, believe it or not, on that cold, damp, overcast afternoon, the sun finally came out!

"Penny Lane is in my ears and in my eyes there beneath the blue suburban skies."

The rest of the trip was a bust. They had knocked down the famous Cavern Club. It wasn't a place to go to without someone showing you the way. Maps to all the key places didn't exist yet.

I thanked my new pal and over the years we stayed in touch. He'd send me little tidbits for my collection. I was hoping he'd make it to the States one day.

Back in London, I headed over to Abbey Road to cross the street in bare feet.

It was too damn cold! I never got my shoes off!

A few weeks later, as we neared Christmas, I was in my office in NYC when the phone rang. It was the gal who got me the job at Capitol Records. She had moved to Los Angeles to work at the Tower and subsequently was hired by one of the biggest public relations companies in the world.

I picked up the phone and said hello.

"Dave, I told one of our clients you just got back from Liverpool. He was wondering what you did there as a Beatles fan. I was thinking you might be able to help him?"

"Sure!" I said.

"Dave, say hello to Michael Jackson."

GULP! "Hi Michael," I said.

"Hi David, I'm doing a concert in Liverpool during my Bad Tour and I'm wondering what to do while I'm there. I want it to be special," he said.

It was like a sock lodged in my throat when I tried to speak coherently.

I ran it down to him and wished him good luck!

Later, when he played his Bad Tour in Liverpool, he went off script and his band did a Beatles medley that included "Day Tripper," "Taxman," "I Want to Hold Your Hand," "Eleanor Rigby," "Yellow Submarine," "Drive My Car," "Lady Madonna" and ended with "Let It Be."

Chapter 45

Slam Dunks From Duane Eddy &
Paul Shaffer

After we tried our luck with Ricky Nelson doing contemporary songs, Capitol tried their luck on Duane Eddy. Duane was a twanging guitar player that had been making records since 1962. His albums included titles like "Have 'Twangy' Guitar Will Travel," The 'Twangs' the Thang," "$1,000,000.00 Worth of Twang," "Twistin' with Duane Eddy," "Twistin' 'N' Twangin," Twangin Up a Storm!" and "Duane-a-Go-Go." The man tried everything, including "Duane Eddy does Bob Dylan" back in 1965!

In 1987, Capitol flew me out to the Tower to hear the new record called "Duane Eddy" in Studio B with guests that included John Fogerty and Brian Setzer. Before they played the record, Duane told us he was able to put together an all star cast of players including Paul McCartney, George Harrison, Jeff Lynne plus guitar champs James Burton, Steve Cropper and John Fogerty. In one of the most entertaining tracks called "The Trembler," Duane plays with Ravi Shankar.

I thought we'd light up the airwaves but we didn't. Nobody cared for it. It was a stiff.

A few years later, TV talk show host David Letterman's sidekick, Paul Shaffer, put out an album on Capitol with some of his friends. It sounded like a winner on paper. Paul had vocals on his record that included Carole King, Dion, Johnny Maestro, Darlene Love, Mavis Staples, and Ellie Greenwich. He had the very best players to help the record gel. He had Allen Toussaint, Donald "Duck" Dunn, Steve Cropper, Don Covay, Ben E King, Bobby Womack, and Wilson Pickett. He also had guests like Mick Fleetwood, Dick Dale, Joe Satriani, Joe Walsh, Brian Wilson and Buddy Guy. He had Eric Burdon, Koko Taylor, George Clinton, Valerie Simpson and David Sanborn.

I was surprised he never promoted the album on the "Late Night With David Letterman."

Paul was a fun guy to hang around. He always had the best pot!

He could have been a promotion man too!

With a cast of thousands, a Capitol recording contract and a late-night show reaching millions, it was nevertheless a grand stiff.

Chapter 46

Merv

Merv was the billygoat of the staff. He'd been there forever and held titles like salesman, branch manager and, finally, promotion manager in Hartford, Connecticut. Most companies had no promo man there but Merv was family. He was special. He was also a curmudgeon who marched to his own beat. He was always outspoken and sometimes that got him in trouble. But he was a pro. Most of the staff was in their mid-twenties. Merv was closing in on 70 and had the balls to wear a leather sleeveless Iron Maiden jacket.

Merv was a trip!

The first time I met him, he busted me. He was leaving a radio station the same time I was. He worked at Capitol and I was somewhere else. I was in a mad rush to get back to NYC and he caught me in the parking lot and asked me if I ever heard of the Motels. I hadn't and didn't give a shit but I said yes, I'd heard them. He said, "Did you hear the new album?" and I said "yes" just to keep moving so I could get out of there. "No, you haven't! It's not out yet! You haven't heard this one! You want a copy? I have one in my trunk." I said, "No thanks, not today, I have to go." "Wait a minute, you're a promotion man, right? You like hit records, right? Come with me and take one. You gotta have it." I really didn't care but now he had me in the palm of his hand, heading to his car to get an album I don't want. Now that's a good promo man!

Once at Capitol, Iron Maiden had a contest where the winning promo person got to go to Japan for three weeks and bring a guest. All you had to do was to come up with a good Iron Maiden idea. I decided to go to a famous tattoo parlor in the city and have him put the Iron Maiden logo of Eddie the Monster on my arm. I wanted it real big and good looking and temporary! I didn't win but had a lot of fun doing it. However, Merv won the contest.

He worked with one of his rock stations to have a kid come down with the heaviest metal he could carry. On the day of the contest, this kid came around the corner of the station carrying a full-blown Chevy 8 engine transmission on his shoulders. It was fantastic.

If he thought a record was a stiff, he'd say, "That record wasn't released, it escaped!"

If it was a tough record and wasn't behaving like a hit, he'd tell the boss, "It'll take an act of Congress to break that fuckin' record!"

I couldn't get enough of Merv. When I arrived at his house for the first time, his wife Sylvia made coffee while Merv and I hunted everywhere possible to try to find a Beatle Butcher cover he might have stashed away.

I came away empty!

Chapter 47

Fast Forward 1986

I t was now October and the full pressure was on the promotion team to deliver this year's hits for the big upcoming holiday season when most of our product is sold. It was a huge battle for the top of the *Billboard* charts being fought by the likes of Tina Turner "Typical Male" from "Break Every Rule," Cyndi Lauper "True Colors" from the album of the same name on Epic Records and Janet Jackson "When I Think Of You" from her album "Control" on A&M Records. Three different record companies, all with a plan to take over the top of the chart.

It wasn't a great time to be on a call with Mr. Cattle Prod. You could smell that rumpdog coming after us. I grabbed a mug of coffee and closed the door to my office. After a few smoker chokes, a quick roll call and we were off.

He began. "Tina Turner is #2 in Billboard!!! Unless we get our collective asses in gear real quick Cyndi

Lauper will be looking at Tina Turner right out her rear-view mirror!!!!! THIS AIN'T ACCEPTABLE!!! Not good! Not good at all!!! Janet Jackson is a big R&B record as is the Tina Turner. Cyndi Lauper is not an R&B record and it's blowing right past us!!!! What we need to do next week is GET MORE HOT REPORTS! We are down 14 hot reports from last week!!! That's the pits!!! We need to get outstanding chart jumps from every radio station playing Tina!!!! We had 26 same [no upward or backward move on the radio station playlist] and four downs this week!!! THIS IS NOT ACCEPTABLE UNLESS THE SAME WAS A #1 AND STAYED THERE! We will not have four downs next week!!!! I will only accept a "same" if the station freezes their list! We need to put distance between us and Cyndi Lauper!!! WE ARE NOT GOING TO ACCEPT A #2 RECORD!!!!! WE WILL MAKE THIS RECORD #1!!! There are winners and losers and #2 is a loser!!!! #1 is a WINNER!!!! We will not lose!!!! No excuses!!!

"We got a new plan on the Crowded House. We can get a break at radio! Rock, top 40 and modern rock ain't there! So, like Elektra did with Simply Red's, 'Holding Back The Years', we're gonna have to start it at adult contemporary formats. There was no top 40 play on Simply Red. It was not a top 15 pop record that adult contemporary picked up on. They led the way!! It was a top 15 at adult contemporary track before top 40 played it!! There is no reason why Crowded House can't get adult contemporary acceptance. Let's get this record started! We made a big deal to drill this thing in on the Gavin Report tip sheet small stations. We already have 18 stations on board! As soon as we get 20 stations, the Gavin Report will give us a 'record to watch' tip to the programmers, which will put the record in print again!! We'll have those next week. We THINK it's a hit! We've got our sales guys calling accounts! Radio people that are playing it are liking it! We're giving away singles to the indie stores!

"Okay, here's the great Seger update. You're all going to get copies of the Bob Seger reviews of the New York City shows. The most jaded city in America says the show is spectacular!!! I want Los Angeles, Chicago, Dallas, and San Francisco to make copies and send them to every station next week. Put a cover note explaining Bob did FOUR SOLD OUT SHOWS IN NEW YORK CITY! He really tore it up!!!

"While I've got you all on the call I wanna talk about rock radio. Completely disappointing this week!!!! The Tina Turner is #4, stuck behind Bryan Adams!! The McCartney is starting to erode!!! We have a 12" coming next week from 'Press To Play' called 'Stranglehold.' Let's go back to radio and pound it hard!! We have a new Steve Miller Band 12" coming called 'I Wanna Make The World Turn Around' from his new album 'Living In The 20th

Century.'" (Eventually the Steve Miller Band would go to #1 for six weeks on the rock charts.)

"We need to continue to stress rock & roll records in terms of what's happening with metal records. I think we have some pleasant surprises. Megadeth is now in full time rotation at WBCN in Boston and WXRK in New York City. Megadeth's career can mirror Iron Maiden! In fact, it's already off to a quicker start than Iron Maiden. Iron Maiden's first album sold only 25,000 for the life of the record. Megadeth's first album is almost 100,000 in the first three weeks!!! This debut album could be a gold album!! It could be as big as the Metallica record on Elektra. We have to get feature play converted to full time play wherever it's getting played. Maximize the feature play as much as possible.

"With Great White, Saxon, Alcatraz and Poison on the road, you have to make sure you have your towns covered! You have to work closely with the branch managers, the salesmen, and the customer service representative to try to make an event of the situation! We need BIG EVENTS! We need stores aware of the tour with in-store merchandising. We need to make sure radio is aware. We need to make sure local writers are aware! Look at Bon Jovi. There's a band that's been around a long time and they developed and developed and developed and along the way they sold a lot of records! They developed a big fan base and they made an accessible record. Now they're going to have a top 10 single with 'You Give Love A Bad Name' and a double platinum album 'Slippery When Wet.' That didn't happen overnight. It was a five-year process. I don't know if Great White or Saxon or Alcatraz is the next Bon Jovi but I know we have to go out there and go for it! With a new Tina Turner or a new Duran Duran album the only question is how many are you going to ship? With developing projects, we have to roll up our sleeves and grind it out.

"Next Tuesday everyone will receive the new Duran Duran single 'Notorious.' I want you to hand deliver it Wednesday! Set up overnight delivery so by Wednesday at noon there are 237 top 40 stations onboard! I WANT TO BLOW IT UP IN THE BLINK OF AN EYE!"

Duran Duran was now a three-piece band after two members left. Like the Tina Turner, the single ended up at #2 – behind the Bangles "Walk Like An Egyptian" on the *Billboard* Hot 100.

Chapter 48

#2 Stinks!

M r. Cattle Prod didn't want any call and responses on his weekly calls. You were better off keeping your mouth shut. The weekly calls were at their worst if the rumpdog just came from the President's office. It's one thing to just shit on us, but once in awhile he'd go around the horn and, if you weren't prepared, WATCH OUT!

It was early in October of 1986. Tina Turner, Janet Jackson and Cyndi Lauper were still battling it out for the top spot on the *Billboard* Hot 100 in the highly competitive fourth quarter. Janet Jackson's "When I Think of You" was at #3, while Tina's "Typical Male" moved from #16 to #8 and Cyndi Lauper's "True Colors" jumped 17-10.

As usual, I grabbed a pot of coffee for my office and put my feet on the desk.

The call began.

"Unless we do something about it, we'll end up with a #2 record! We're not going to settle for anything

less than a #1 for Tina Turner!!! We're not gonna
settle for a #2!!! WE WILL HAVE A #1 RECORD!!!
Next week, every station you talk to needs to give
us hot reports and make damn well sure this record
moves up everywhere!!! We need a big week at radio!
We need number ones! We need chart jumps and
hot reports!! I don't know about you, but I'm gonna
have a hell of a time looking my boss in the eye if
we don't get to #1!!! I don't want to tell him we're
#2!!!! I don't want to tell him we're the #2 guys!!! We
can't get #1 records with Tina Turner!! You better
look at your stats and analyze it and if need be, ask
for favors!!!! Pat the guy on the back, kick him in the
ass!!! Whatever it is that gets the jumps next week, do
it!!! Is that clear?

"Let's go over it," he barked.

"Hey Miami!!! I see Y100 went #4-#3. You've got
to make sure it goes #3-#1 next week!!! WINZ went
4-4 but he did give you a hot report! He's a good guy.
Next week you got to move up!!

"Hey Boston!!! WXKS took us #5-#2 with a hot
report so let's twist him to go #2-#1 with a hot report!!

"Hey Cincinnati!!! At Q102 we went #26-#23!!!!
What the fuck is that!!!!!!"

The local Cincinnati guy softly squeaked, "That's
a good jump for that station."

"MY ASS!!!!! A 3-point jump when you're in the
fucking 20's???

The guy gulped and said, "They're very slow with their chart."

"Well, if I wanted to take the time and look at his fucking chart, I'll bet you Cyndi Lauper is doing a hell of a lot better on their chart!!!!"

Cincinnati replied, "He just added Cyndi last week!"

That knocked the wind out of the blowhard. After he caught his breath, he continued with the call.

"The rest of you people better know where you stand with the Tina Turner!!! We have to take Tina to #1! That's what it comes down to. You don't stop at #2! You don't let CBS stick it up our ass!!!!"

By the end of the year, Cyndi and Janet both hit #1. Despite our best efforts, we stalled at #2 with Tina.

"We had a marvelous week on Billy Squier with three adds on the brand new track 'Love Is The Hero.' Have we given up on this record? Are we still breathing? Are we gonna get some action on this record or not? Our rock activity this week was dick. Top 40 activity on Billy Squier is an embarrassment. If we do that next week, we may as well go and take all the records back and say we made a mistake releasing the record. Gimme a break!!!!"

"What's the problem with getting this record played?" asked the boss.

"Hey Miami, how you doing?"

"I got all medium rotations but I shouldn't have any problems getting at least 3-4 into heavy rotation next week," the local guy in Florida replied.

"That's the spirit, Miami! Accept the mediums and accept the number two's!!!!"

"Absolutely not," cried the local guy.

"That's the way to win in life!!!" the boss yelled at him.

"I don't want this record lollygagging around the bottom 20 of the rock charts! I want to make damn well sure that this is a top 5 rock track. We need this to sell some damn records and get this guy out on the road. We have failed miserably. This is as embarrassing as Tina Turner not going #1. So, we have two potential major embarrassments here!!!

"Let's go around the horn and see what top 40's we can get on Billy Squier.

"Miami? What happened to WINZ this week? I thought you were close."

"They are close. We just didn't get them. We'll have them next week," the promo guy said.

The boss snapped back, "You think so after we had a three add week???"

"Well, I gotta keep trying," the local guy said.

"Or do you think the guy is gonna sit back and say wait a second, I think this record just crumbled this past week!! It only had three adds!!!"

"That's a possibility," said the promo man.

"Possibility????? You know what pal? I'm telling you it's a fucking probability!!!!!!!!"

"Yeah, well, I gotta go in and fight for it," cried the promo man, begging to get off the hook.

"It ain't gonna be there!!!!

"You gotta beat the bushes. You gotta find two secondaries to get this record on. We're in business with this record. We gotta ramp this record up to 100 stations in the coming weeks. We need a story to tell! Get some damn stations! Quality stations!"

Squier's single ended up dying a quick death after peaking at #80 in Billboard.

"Freddie Jackson's 'Tasty Love' is an R&B smash!!! It's the lead single from his new album 'Just Like The First Time.'

"Hey Boston! We got Providence!! Where's Sonny at WXKS in Boston with this record?"

"I thought we were getting him this week, but he didn't come in. I think I forgot to bring my kneepads to blow him! We should have him for next week," the Boston guy snickered.

"Bring in the kneepads, bring in a baseball bat, buy a cattle prod! We need Sonny on this record!!!

"The record is top 10 on the R&B airplay charts and top 20 in the R&B sales charts. I want you to talk to your sales force about escalating the sales reports!!! Make sure this record pops fast. Be in everyone's face on Monday!! This record is happening quicker than you think!! Go through the tap dance and show them the *Billboard* numbers.

"Make up a fuckin' story! Tell a fuckin' lie!!! We've been doing it all our lives!!! I want the Freddie Jackson on!!! We NEED this record! If we don't bring this record in, all of our hard work of a year ago is flushed down the toilet. We'll have to go back and start all over again.

"Freddie Jackson goes from nothing to superstar to a nobody overnight! We gotta get it started NOW! We had three adult contemporary adds on Freddie Jackson. I think we could all understand Tina Turner not being a big adult contemporary record, but Freddie Jackson is a ballad!!! Last time I checked on some of these stations I noticed they play a lot of ballads. A lot of soft records. Do we take the time to talk to adult contemporary stations once in a while? I'd appreciate it if we could do that.

"Talk to them about Freddie Jackson! Talk to them about Crowded House!! Make it a point next week to talk to adult contemporary stations.

"I know our guy in Hartford's time is too valuable to be mailing records, licking stamps and closing envelopes. We want him out at adult contemporary radio stations working Crowded House, right Merv?"

Merv pipes in with a gruff voice. "I will not discuss the Crowded House 'cause it's a HIT RECORD!! It's also a very frustrating record and I don't blame you one bit!!!"

"Are you gonna lead the way on this record?" Mr. Cattle Prod asked.

"I've been trying to lead the way and it's very frustrating!!! Especially because it's an adult contemporary record, but I am close on a couple of stations. I'm not gonna give up on the damn thing and I agree with you 1000%!!!" the Hartford guy explained.

"Well, I think it's time for a veteran like you to step up and show us how to do it! Lead the way," the boss snarled back.

Merv replied, "I don't know about that, but I've been trying. Boy, you talk about frustration, that record is a hit!!!"

The boss completely lost it and screamed back at him.

"Frustration!!!!!!! Talk about frustration!!!! I'll tell you about frustration!!! Frustration is sitting in the Capitol Tower in a room on Wednesday afternoon with 42 people and having the President ask you what's going on at radio. What's going on with Billy Squier, with Freddie Jackson, with Crowded House? That's what frustration is! And asking is Tina Turner gonna go to #1? That's what frustration is!!!!!"

"You're in the hot seat," Merv replied.

"FUCK THE HOT SEAT! The hot seat doesn't bother me! The results, that's what bothers me!!!"

Merv wasn't done. "May I say one thing? As long as you asked me. You're right about Tina, you're right about Jackson, you're right about Crowded House, but the Squier record is a tough top 40 record for me. I've got three stations playing it and one is looking at it. It's KC101 in New Haven and the guy wants me to call him back. He'll ask me how many adds did Squier get this week and when I tell him three, he's gonna balk. He's been looking at the damn record but he's got a consultant who ain't crazy about Billy Squier. When I tell him we got only three adds, and we're going after the record, which I've been telling him, that's a very tough negative thing!!!"

"YOU GOT IT, MERV!" Mr. Cattle Prod screamed at him.

"WE GOT THREE ADDS AND WE'RE GOING AFTER IT!!!! WE'RE STORMING THE BEACH IN NORMANDY!!!!"

"It's not the best record on the album and YOU KNOW IT!!!," Merv barked back.

"THAT'S YOUR OPINION!!!," the rumpdog shouted.

"No, it's a lot of people's opinion!!!!!," Merv blew back at him.

"BLOW IT OUR YOUR ASS, MERV!!!!!

"YOUR NOT AN A&R MAN!!!!" Mr.Cattle Prod was bellowing.

"YES, I AM!!!!," Merv shouted back.

"NO, YOU'RE NOT PAL!!!!!

"I have a right to my opinion," Merv barked.

"You may have a right to your opinion, but you keep your damn opinion to yourself!!!! You don't

EVER, EVER say that another song is better on the album!!! You've just given a radio station an excuse not to play the track!"

"I didn't say it to radio. I said it to you!"

"Don't say it to me! Because if you say it to me, you may slip and say it to someone else."

"Okay, I'm sorry I brought it up," he retreated.

"You're damn right you're sorry you brought it up!!! You just got ZAPPED on your quarterly review for that one!!!"

"When we're in the Tower and we talk about single choices for radio, a lot of thought and time goes into the process. There are a lot of reasons why a particular track is chosen at a particular time for the first or second or third single. Trust me, we are not going to pick singles by committee!! We're not gonna have 23 people vote on singles!! You do that and we'll never get a damn decision around here!!! And unlike the guy that was here before me, I listen to records and that IS the best first Squier single for across the board radio approach!!!!

"With Paul McCartney at rock radio we had erosion this week!!! You'll be getting a 12" on 'Stranglehold.' I'd like to turn that erosion around!!! Let's get the bullet back on the track!!! In a couple of weeks, when we release the 7" single to top 40 radio, we'll have a nice rock base.

"On the Bob Seger, you'll be getting a 12" on the song 'Miami.' You go to rock radio with all of the fire and all of the enthusiasm you can muster and let's get another top 10 rock track!!!!

"Iron Maiden have one of the hottest selling albums at retail!!! We're starting to get some rock stations to give us a full time shot at airplay!!! WXRK in New York came in last week and we got WBCN in Boston this week!!! I want you to continue to pound, continue to beat down everybody!! The stations have got to be picking up the retail action as well!!! Get those target stations that are going to give us metal shop feature airplay!!! Get as much exposure as possible!!! We're at 600,000 albums in three weeks!!! One of the catalog albums just went Platinum!!!! One of them is close to Platinum and another one is close to Gold!!!! We could conceivably, in the next 60 days, have every Iron Maiden album, except for the very first one, to be released Gold or Platinum!!! Not bad!!!!! When they come over and tour in January, they will sell out 15,000 seats everywhere they play!!! The catalog is gonna take off and we could end up selling, between the new album and the past releases, a million and a half more Iron Maiden albums!!!! Let's maximize this premier metal band.

"So, does anyone have any questions about what we're gonna do about our current records?

"Let's recap! Tina gonna go #1? Billy Squier's gonna have a good week at top 40 and rock? We gonna get Freddie Jackson started next week at top

40 and adult contemporary? Crowded House adds at adult contemporary next week?

"Then let's aggressively go out there and get Seger's 'Miami,' the new McCartney 12"!! Is that very clear?

"Now next Tuesday you'll be receiving your Duran Duran 7"and a 12" single. The song is called "Notorious." They are just completing the video and they're in New York finishing up their studio album. John Taylor and Nick Rhodes have agreed to give us a couple of hours to do phoners to radio stations, so give some thought of whom you want them to call. There is a possibility that for the November tour we can set up contests for radio and fly the winners someplace to meet these three Duran characters. I'll keep you posted!

"That's it! NOW GET TO WORK!!!! I'll be back after lunch if you need me!"

Chapter 49

We're Loaded Up!

It was early November in '86, just a few weeks from the big Thanksgiving and Christmas sales season. Everyone at Capitol was on their toes and focused for the busy few weeks ahead.

Mr. Cattle Prod waited until Sunday evening at 8:00 p.m. on the East Coast to spill the beans on the upcoming week. I sharpened my pencil and poured a big glass of wine.

When the phone rang, I could instantly hear the gruff of the rumpdog.

"Let's begin!" he barked.

"On the Freddie Jackson 'A Little Bit More' we picked up 10 top 40 stations this week. We have a good profile now. We have the #1 R&B track and it's selling! The album is selling too! We're #2 in Atlanta! The south will fall next week and then we will spill into New Orleans and Texas. We sold over 600,000 records in two weeks!! We need more stations!!!

"Steve Miller's 'I Want To Turn The World Around' was the big disappointment at top 40 radio this week. We need to muscle up!!! Where the song is on the radio, we have to chart!!! Where we are charted, we need to move up!!! This is a classic upper demo record!!! The reaction is phenomenal!!!! It's a smash!!!

"The 'Miami' track from Bob Seger had a good first week at top 40. We had 10 big adds and a debut in the *Billboard* Hot 100. We need to re-energize this track at rock radio. Take a look around and see what stations took a pass or are on the fence. Some programmers say they don't want to stick their necks out. Go back and show them 'Miami' was one of the most-added records. Point to the tour success and the amount of tickets he's selling. Bob's manager will give us front row tickets for adds! Set up guitar giveaways with stations! Give away CD players! Give away tour jackets!! Give away tickets!! Analyze your stats and call and pitch the radio stations again!! You've got to push this through the system!!! We're selling millions and the tour has yet to go west of the Mississippi!! We're going into the Christmas season and we'll sell another million units. That's our mission in life!!

"The Paul McCartney track 'Stranglehold' had a great week but we have to do a couple of things. Obviously, everyone who added the Bob Seger didn't add the McCartney, so look at your stats. Between

Freddie Jackson, Steve Miller, and Paul McCartney we have to get two adds from all your top 40 stations. It's the only way we're gonna keep the momentum going. With McCartney you have to recognize the airplay we've got at the rock stations. We'll have special McCartney CDs for rock radio coming, so go out there with a passion!

"By the way, I got a call from one of our staff in the field today. He was at a tiny pee wee third tier small radio station. He said, 'I gave the guy a CD player, then I gave him a tour jacket, and then I gave him an autographed guitar and THEN I gave him CDs to give away!!!'"

"For a small station, you gave away the whole store?"

"Yeah!!! But he added Bob Seger!!"

"Big deal!"

"Well, he also added Paul McCartney!!!"

"Ah, not bad."

"Well, he also added Steve Miller!!!"

"Jeesh, ya got three?"

"Well, he also added the Freddie Jackson!!!!!"

"Four adds?"

"Well, not exactly. He added the Crowded House too!!!!!!"

"Now I've been in this business more years than I want to admit. Even in my wildest bullshit stories, I would never make up a story about five adds on a small station at one time, but you pulled the brass ring for this one. A five-banger!!!!!!

"Alright, let's move to the new Tina Turner single, 'Back Where You Started.' This is a smash! IT HAS TO BE THE #1 MOST ADDED RECORD NEXT WEEK! We need 100-150 adds next week!!!!! Roll up your sleeves 'cause you also got to deliver on Freddie, Steve Miller and McCartney!!!!

"On 'Notorious' by Duran Duran we have too many one-point jumps. We're on over 200 stations and we need to turn that around! We NEED 6 POINT JUMPS!!! We only have 14 hot reports! We gotta start building those hot reports!!! Granted, we're only starting our third week on the record, but we need to ram this record through as quickly as possible! Duran's records usually don't have long lives. They usually burn out fast, around eight weeks!! There will be a new Duran Duran I'm picking right now. It will be ready the first week of January since 'Notorious' won't be around in mid-January. A week from Friday, we ship the new album called 'Notorious.' We're looking to ship a million plus units. The hotter the single, the easier it is to get albums into the stores.

"Also, on our plate is Crowded House. We have a full plate so we'll pick a day to discuss our blitz. Don't overlook it! It won't go away!! Work it at the adult contemporary format! We can't overlook it!

"Let's talk about covering concerts. The group Fetchin' Bones were in Atlanta and nobody covered the show!! In Raleigh, no one covered the show. In New York City, everybody was there! If you can't make the show, call the manager. Tell him you can't be there cause it's 300 miles away. Ask your district manager if someone can cover the show. Why is no one covering development acts? Make sure the act is covered!

"Okay, let's focus on the rock part of the call. Let's close out Steve Miller Band and go to #1. The Bob Seger needs tonnage! For the McCartney we have a special CD for you to give away. The new John Lennon album 'Menlove Avenue' is NOT A PRIORITY but 'Rock & Roll People' is getting sporadic play." [It was an album of outtakes from John's 'Walls & Bridges' and 'Rock n' Roll' albums.]

"Poison is on the Ratt tour (Rat-Poison!). Poison's second or third album could well beat 350,000 sales! Polygram has built a good image on Def Leopard, Rush, Bon Jovi and Cinderella. For Iron Maiden and W.A.S.P., we have a good image too. It's not due to heavy airplay, but because of their tours, press, merchandising, enthusiasm and understanding of the music! Megadeth is NEXT!

"You have to know the difference between W.A.S.P., Iron Maiden, Poison and Saxon. We've got an expert out here in the Tower!! He runs the rock department. His name is Ray Tusken and he's the expert!! If you take a look at him, he's fried from listening to that SHIT! That's why he's an expert!!!!!

"Didja know Saxon is one of my all-time favorite bands? The manager called me and asked me go see the show. It was cold, it was raining, and I felt shitty. I'm back of the stage and the band is playing. The kids are holding up matches. The noise is bedlam! The kids are screaming, 'HEY MOTHERFUCKERS!!! ROCK & ROLL!!!' The bass player comes around the drums on the riser and walks by the side of the stage. I try to say something but he doesn't hear me so I reach out to grab him and he falls off the fuckin' stage!!!! RIGHT ON THE FLOOR! BOOM!!!!! CRASH!!!! I'm starting to laugh. The band goes 'Let's go back on. Where's Dobby?' I point to the floor. It's about a five-foot drop. They're all looking from the stage and Dobby is cold cocked and out like a light! Somebody goes down and slaps his face and props him up and wipes him with a cold towel and gets him back up on the stage. 'I think I broke my leg!!' he screams. 'Come on Dobby!!! One more song!!' So, he limps on the stage for the closing song then is rushed to a car and over to the hospital!!! Before all of us at Capitol left the building, Dobby came back!!! His leg was in a full cast!!! Go see them!! Maybe you'll be fortunate and see them fall off the stage!!"

Chapter 50

"GO BACK TO YOUR STALL,
YOU'RE DOG MEAT"

The head of publicity came to my office waving a piece of paper in her hand. She looked rattled and her face had turned white. She was shaking when the paper fell and landed on my desk. It was a fax from Los Angeles.

Variety was reporting a story that began with the words:

"Go back to your stall, you're dog meat!"

I laughed and wondered what the hell could this be about.

The headline was, "Promo Exec At Capitol Sues Colleague."

It read, "The national album promotion manager director of Capitol Records has sued a vice president for allegedly repeatedly attacking him with a cattle prod, insulting him, and forcing him to take a substantial cut in pay."

How was this possible? I was on the phone with both of them at least twice a day, and had traveled with both, separately. I had never heard a peep about this encounter.

Capitol promotion staff had JUST gotten over the "new payola" scandal. The one that Brian Ross reported on NBC news. The opening footage of the earth-shaking music scandal showed a Capitol promo executive with a known underworld figure!

This business really was getting CRAZY! And DANGEROUS!

The *Variety* article continued. I was hanging on every word.

"Bill Bartlett, in a complaint filed in Los Angeles Superior Court, claims that Walter Lee, Capitol's senior vice president of promotion and marketing, first poked him with the prod last May 14 and said, 'You're dog meat. Go back to your stall.'"

Wow! That was worth re-reading. I was wondering if everyone in the Tower knew about it. My head was spinning. May 14 of last year? It was going on that long and nobody knew?

The article continued.

"There allegedly were more attacks over the next two weeks. Lee also at one point told Barlett that he would be the 'fall guy' in an investigation of payments to disc jockeys for air time, the suit says."

Bill and I were "wine and cheese party planners" according to Walter so it would be hard for me to believe he could pin the payola probe on the rock department. The Feds were looking into top 40 pay-offs, not the album cut, FM stations, who weren't taking anything.

I liked both of these men. Bill started in January of 1980, just like me, and rose up the ranks. He went from a regional promotion person to a national person, just like myself. He made his way out to L.A. to coordinate the priorities to the staff when our buddy Ray became VP of A&R, signing rock bands for the label. A real dream come true for him.

Walter was the big shot VP who came from sales. We knew each other and I'd always be with him when he came to NYC. When he took the job as VP of Promotion, his old friend from Dallas sent Walter a cattle prod with a note saying he may need it in the world of Promotion.

According to the article, Bill asked for a performance review 15 times before getting a fair 6% raise. Over the course of a month in May of 1986, my counterpart said he was poked by a three-foot-long metal cattle prod, which causes electric shocks and burns when it touches human skin. Bill went on to say in court papers that he was harassed, insulted and humiliated, which caused severe mental and emotional suffering.

Apparently, the tension had built over time. These guys were walking the high wire and their nerves were shot. When the new Seger album came out it was up against Van Halen ("5150") and the Rolling Stones ("Dirty Work"). The guy with the cattle prod threatened to fire Bill unless the Seger album reached #1 the following week.

It didn't make it to #1 the following week and he wasn't fired.

By mid-June, the hot head VP said to him, "By the way, the whole cattle prod thing was a big joke."

At the weekly meetings attended by all the other department heads, Bill claimed the VP rejected his priorities for the rock department. He felt insulted. After a two-week medical leave, my counterpart came back to find phone messages from people hearing he was being replaced.

It was true although he did stick around with a major cut in pay for a short while.

Capitol followed up Seger's "American Storm" with "Like A Rock," which peaked at #12 on the *Billboard* Hot 100 and went to #1 on the rock chart. We ended up selling north of three million albums when all was said and done.

Needless to say, the SHIT hit the fan after the *Variety* article ran. By the end of the year, the President of the company was replaced and soon the big VP would take a plunge.

Chapter 51

The Iron Maiden Riot

I ron Maiden came to the New Jersey Meadowlands – then known as the Brendan Byrne Arena – in 1987 to support their new album "Somewhere On Tour." Earlier in the day, their manager Rod, brought Bruce Dickinson, the lead singer, over to my house for a good old fashioned American BBQ. After a case of beer and a few steaks, we all headed to the show.

The band – named after the medieval torture device – loved living up to their reputation of loud guitars, throbbing bass and powerful vocals. Their mascot "Eddie" was a violent subhuman their fans loved.

20,000 fans were ecstatic!

It was a terrific beginning to an extraordinary evening!

Backstage it was mellow with a few more beers being passed around.

Outside the arena was where the trouble began. The fans started throwing and smashing beer bottles in the parking lot.

When the band took the stage, the kids in the cheap seats began to throw firecrackers. Fans were fighting by the stage when Bruce, the lead singer, screamed, "People at Iron Maiden shows DON'T FIGHT!!!"

You could feel the angst. The tension was tight.

The show ended in a frenzy with their great closer "Running Free."

After the show I was backstage tipping the champagne bottle with Rod and the guys.

When I exited the building an hour later, all hell had broken loose. We couldn't believe our eyes. The parking lot was bedlam. There were cars overturned and on fire. The kids were throwing shit on the flames to keep it going. Car windows were getting shattered. State Police cars were showing up.

The fans were throwing bottles at the firemen who responded to the car fires. One officer was injured when a kid backed his car into him.

Two thousand people were still hanging out. News accounts said that over 30 people were arrested for criminal mischief, creating a disturbance, aggravated assault with a car and more.

When Iron Maiden returned to the venue in subsequent years, there were no such incidents. With songs that typically ran over 10 minutes long, the band never charted big radio hits, but has nonetheless managed to sell over 100 million albums worldwide. Their 2019 "Legacy of the Beast" outing ranked in the top 25 of Pollstar's Worldwide Ticket Sales Top 100 tours chart and sold more tickets than artists like Paul McCartney, Zac Brown Band and Travis Scott. *Rolling Stone* described the band's performance of trademark track "The Trooper" at New York City's Barclays Center as "pure multimedia spectacle, absurd yet undeniably awesome – in other words, Iron Maiden in a nutshell." Still managed by Rod Smallwood, Iron Maiden remains one of the most successful yet down-to-earth bands out there.

Chapter 52

Random Notes Christmas 1987

For the Christmas holidays, I thought it would cool to send the great radio folks I'd met over the years some fun, rare Beatle tapes.

I stuck a note inside which said:

"Happy Holidays!!

Every year we give gifts of wine, liquor, garment bags, calculators, sweatshirts, etc.

BORING!!!

This year I've decided to go into the archives and pull out some real gems that cover their entire career including some very interesting solo tapes.

I hope you enjoy this special gift from me to you and have as much fun listening as I had making it!!"

It was on official Capitol letterhead and the tapes were manufactured by Capitol, too!

I had asked my boss Ray if it was cool, and he said, "HELL YEAH."

It was a terrific hit. Most programmers I'd met loved the Beatles, so when we got together in hotel

rooms, cars or at their offices or homes, we really hit
it off. The tape gave me great credibility and made
them more than happy to hear our Capitol product.
Billboard even took note of it, writing:

"Major Beatles maniac and Capitol representative Dave Morrell played Fab Santa by digging
into his own archives while looking for an original
Christmas gift. Morrell's solution: 'Beatle Bits for
Christmas,' a cassette of gems by the group and by
its individual members during the Beatles lifespan."

I got a letter from the 'House Hippy' at Apple
Records - my old friend Richard Dilello, who wrote
The Longest Cocktail Party, an insider look at Apple
Records.

He wrote, "Dear Dave, Thanks a million for
your very thoughtful Christmas gift. The Fabs never
sounded better. Hope all is well with you!"

Then the holiday cards began to arrive.

I received one from the group Heart.

"Dear Dave - Thank you for everything you have
done to make our record such a fantastic success.
It could never have happened without you! We wish
you a very happy new year from all of us. We love
you, Ann, Nancy, Howie, Denny and Mark."

Then I got a card from a duo who called themselves the House of Schock.

"Roll it '87 - Rock it '88!! Happy holidays from
the House of Schock." They were Gina Schock and
Vance De Generes. Gina was the ex-drummer of the

Go Go's and Vance was Ellen's brother. These two snobs came to New York and I took them to lunch with WNEW's PD Scott Muni. All they had to do was smile and thank him, but they couldn't bring themselves to speak a single word during our hour-long lunch. Before the check came, their career in New York was officially over. Kaput! I stuffed them in a cab like I was shoving them in a casket. I never mentioned them or the record ever again.

Chapter 53

Rock & Roll Hall of Fame 1988

The big boss wasn't coming to New York to attend the Rock & Roll Hall of Fame induction ceremony, so the hottest ticket ever was now available to me. It was official that I could go to see the Beatles get inducted. The ceremony would take place in the hotel ballroom of the famed Waldorf-Astoria hotel.

Capitol had two tables – one for the heavyweights, which included the President and his top guests, and a second for the peons. One of the tables was up close in the middle of the room next to a Motown table and near the Beach Boys table, while the other table was way in the back near the exit and bathrooms.

I came prepared for the evening. I rented a tux with a big cummerbund and it was there I put a tiny tape recorder so I could tape the live music. I was contemplating bringing the Beatles Butcher cover with me. I had John's signature on it, Paul's signature on it and Ringo signed it, too. I just needed George's autograph. I ditched the idea since I wasn't sure you could bring anything into the ballroom.

When I arrived, I was surprised to be seated up close. I stood up to gaze at the room. Right next to my chair was Berry Gordy, the chairman of Motown Records and the writer of the great song "Money" that the Beatles covered. It was also one of Motown's first hit records.

I looked a little to my right and, low and behold, there were Ringo, George, Dylan and Elton John sitting together. I had to figure out a way to get over there and say hello. At the table with me was the NY office staff. We knew we didn't deserve being here but we sure were cocky at our good luck. I saw the champagne bottle in the middle of the table and poured myself a glass. I made my way over to George Harrison. I'd never met him before, but I'd seen George perform twice with the Beatles, and I was fortunate to be at his "George Harrison and Friends" show at Madison Square Garden, which raised money for the people of Bangladesh. Ringo and Dylan played at that show, too. I also saw George's solo concert a few years later at Madison Square Garden.

George had been putting out special signed, limited edition books of his work through Genesis Publications. They were very expensive, but certainly worth it. His first book was called, "I, Me, Mine," and it was a personal look at all the lyrics he had written on bits of scrap paper and envelopes. Out of 2,000 books, I had number 56. I didn't know it at the time, but he was finishing up another book for Genesis.

My head was spinning while I was thinking about what I was going to say to George. I didn't want to surprise him so I came from his front so he'd see someone and not be disturbed.

He looked up at me and I said, "Hi George, my name is Dave and I bought your wonderful expensive book, 'I, Me, Mine.' I am number 56 and I am looking forward to your next volume."

He reached out his hand and put it in mine. Then he put his other hand over the top of my hand. I could feel his energy shoot through me. I was locked in.

He said, "Hi Dave, I'm so glad you liked my expensive book. I have the new book upstairs in my room. Would you like to see it later?"

Oh my gosh. Did I hear that right? Did George Harrison just ask me to go to his room? I must be dreaming.

"Thank you so much, I'd love to see it. I'll catch up to you after the show. I can't wait to see what's gonna happen this evening."

I was kneeling by George and as I got up, Ringo turned to talk with him. Someone yelled, "How about a photograph?" and all of a sudden Bob Dylan got up and came around to George. The shutter snapped and I realized I was in the picture. The photographer instantly took off, so I never got to run after him and ask him for a print.

Before the show started, I made my way to the back exit where the bathroom was. As I approached the exit sign way in the back, I saw something that jolted me. It was all the big shots at our company sitting in the peanut gallery. It was then I realized there was a mix up with the tables and tickets. At first I was hoping nobody at that table saw me and asked me where my seat was. I kept on going as fast as I could towards the bathroom. When I walked in, there was George Harrison with Jeff Lynne and Scott Muni from WNEW FM. I said hello to Scott and he introduced me to George who told him we had just met. It was great standing among these giants.

Outside the bathroom, two people walked up to George and asked him for an autograph. As soon as the two folks spoke, George cut them off and said he was here for fun tonight and didn't want to sign autographs. Whew! I was so glad I didn't have the Butcher cover and have him not sign it. It was the right move for me not to bring it. It wasn't appropriate.

Back inside and sitting in the primo seats, we were ready to be sky rocketed to the heavens. The show was incredible. Tonight they were saluting The Beatles, Bob Dylan, The Beach Boys, The Supremes, The Drifters, Les Paul and more!

Little Richard brought the Supremes on and was a firecracker.

Elton John brought the Beach Boys to the stage and, after a few of the boys spoke, Mike Love took over. He had Mohammad Ali as his guest and in his corner for the evening. After dumping on Paul McCartney and Diana Ross for not being there, he got to his meandering point. He said Mick Jagger was chickenshit to get on stage with the Beach Boys!!

He even crowed, "The Beach Boys did about 180 performances last year. I'd like to see the Mop Tops match that." Mike was unruly and out of control. Later, when Bob Dylan spoke, he mentioned how glad he was the Mike didn't mention him!

I'd covered a lot of ground and seen lots of live music, but being in a small ballroom of a hotel and hearing Bob Dylan sing "Like a Rolling Stone" and Mick Jagger belt out "Satisfaction" was paramount. The ultimate moment came when George sang "I Saw Her Standing There." I never got to see the Beatles sing it live, but I did get to witness Paul singing it, John singing it, and now George singing it with Ringo on drums. I was ten feet away and felt ten feet tall.

Everyone was on stage jamming and you hoped it would never end. I danced and howled and twisted and shouted. It felt like a private party and I was in. I really thought I was dreaming.

Singing and playing along were Mick Jagger, Bruce Springsteen, Billy Joel, Jeff Beck, Bob Dylan, Brian Wilson and tons more!

I turned to my left and saw the whole gang from WNEW FM. I went over to say hello and ran into Mark Chernoff, the PD. We had a long history going back to when he ran WDHA over in Dover, NJ. I'd known Mark a really long time and I'd never seen him this happy. I told him I was taping the live music and he lit up!

Later, Mark and I huddled in a small corner to hear how the tape sounded. It was terrific so Mark asked if WNEW FM could run a portion of it. I was thrilled and said of course. We headed over to the station and broke the tape down to feature small portions of the songs. New York City was going to wake up and hear quite a story.

The following morning, WNEW FM went on the air with this exclusive music taped just hours ago. Nobody in the world could have topped it. It was exciting to hear again, and even more exciting to a part of the WNEW FM family.

I'd been going weekly to visit the station for almost 15 years now and it never got dull or boring.

Back at Capitol, we never heard a peep from the big wigs that got stiffed in the bad seats.

Since the Rock Hall has grown, so have the musical performances. Nowadays, they are held in 20,000 seat arenas and made into TV specials. If John were alive, he would have used his influence to get Larry Williams into the Hall of Fame. Larry wrote "Dizzy Miss Lizzy," "Slow Down," "Bad Boy," "Bony

Moronie," and more. John went on to record all of these songs.

Once, a long time ago, I got a call and John came on the line. He was working on the final song of his "Rock 'n' Roll" album and remembered I had a good collection of 45s. He asked me for a copy of "Just Because" by Larry Williams.

We lost both John and Larry in 1980.

Chapter 54

John Lennon's Star On
The Walk Of Fame

In was September 30, 1988 at 1750 Vine Street, also the home of the Capitol Records Tower, when they held the Walk of Fame ceremony for John Lennon's star. Capitol invited people from all over the country to attend and Yoko was going to be there. We'd be able to have private time with her and everyone would have a photograph taken with her.

Before I arrived in Los Angeles, I called National Car Rental and asked them to hold an oldie convertible for me.

When I arrived I saw the most beautiful car in the world. It was a 1958 red Chevrolet convertible. I was in heaven just standing next to it. I was going to have fun in this head turner. For 40 bucks a day you don't get a showroom model, you get a worn-down car with a good-looking body. The floor pedals were all worn, the dashboard was well worn, in fact, the more I looked at it, the more I realized it actually was a 40 dollar a day car.

The top was down, the engine was humming, and the AM radio dial was tuned to some Mariachi music. I just hoped the brakes and horn worked. I got the old tank up to speed and made my way on to the 405 freeway, heading to Hollywood. While buzzing along on this king size waterbed I heard a horn and looked over. The guy was waving and giving me the thumbs up. I smiled back and tooted my horn to say thanks, but the horn got stuck and was wailing really loud. The guy that waved was now laughing and pulled ahead. I couldn't get the horn to stop blowing so I had to try to get off the highway.

I saw an exit and prayed there be no red light when I pulled off. The horn was blowing loud. Louder than I remember horns being! I got off but couldn't find a gas station so I had to get back on the 405. It was pitiful. My mind was racing. I pulled off the next exit and saw a service station. As I entered, everyone was looking at the car wondering why my hand was blasting the horn. I pulled up and hit the brake and then put my arms in the air like I was giving up and that my hand wasn't on the horn.

A guy in a boiler suit from the service station came running over, waving me off. Shooing me to leave. I had to scream, "Hey mister! The horn is stuck. Do you know how to stop it?" He put his fingers in his ears and gave me a look that said, "Get lost!"

I took off again but this time I pulled over when I saw a phone booth. I remembered my cousin had a Rent-A-Wreck rental car franchise up in Albany, NY. I knew if I got him on the phone and told him my predicament he'd laugh and say, "You're on your own!" and then hang up on me.

I called with the horn blasting. I tried to park it further away from the phone and then I reached my cousin. I used a fake voice and told him a car I rented had a stuck horn. He said, "Yeah, I hear it in the background. Go to the fuse box near the floor in the front driver side and take out the first fuse. It's the master and it will make everything stop." I said thanks and hung up. I never told him it was me. I was very thankful.

I went over to the car and found that fuse. I took it out and the horn stopped. Silence WAS golden. I started the old boat back up and went on my way.

When I got to the hotel I was staying at, I pulled in and heard another car beeping at me. The fellow was giving me the thumbs up. I looked at the guy and noticed it was Kenny Loggins. I was officially in Hollywood! If he'd only known it was a 40-dollar a day beater, he wouldn't have looked twice.

The ceremony was nice but it didn't really move me. The next day, I went back to lay flowers on John's star and reflect privately on what the man and his music had meant to my life. Personally speaking, I don't think John would have cared about a gold star even if it was in front of the Capitol Tower.

After a few days of fun in the sun with the good-looking redhead convertible, I set my alarm to get up early and head to the airport. I was also taking the PD and MD of WMMR in Philadelphia with me. It was still kind of dark out and it was unusually cold for Los Angeles. We got on the 405 and began to get up to speed. It got colder. We decided to pull over and put the top up.

The top wouldn't go up. We tried. We tried hard. We pulled on the fucking piece of shit with all our might and it still wouldn't budge. We got the fuck it's and got back in the car. I was driving and I was shivering. They put the heat on high and ducked down. The faster we went, the colder it was. The slower we got, the longer it would take. We were in a quandary. We kicked the old bomb up to almost 75 miles per hour and felt like skeletons on a pirate ship.

We made it but the cool factor was long gone. We were angry, tired and hungry and just wanted to be home, comfortable in our own beds.

Chapter 55

In The End

Mr. Cattle Prod resigned due to philosophical differences with new president Joe Smith. Joe was a guy I worked with before at Warner Bros. and we always liked each other. He had been a DJ and a promotion man so he was easy to be around. He'd always swing by everyone's office to say hello when he was in town.

Mr. Cattle Prod was good to me. We remained friends to the end.

By the end of my wonderful, 10-year run at Capitol, we had gone through five presidents and more than seven vice presidents of promotion.

A new promo guy came in to rally the troops. He immediately fired the old guard, who had been with the company since the 60s, and replaced them with a bunch of old guys who had reported to him at another company. Those guys called him "The Wild Man."

The title fit him like a glove and he adored it.

After a decade of hearing these VPs of promotion calling us a piece of shit, it's hard to believe another boss could get completely ridiculous and lose all control, but it happened.

Even his own boys couldn't start a record.

The records he wanted on the radio were stiffs. Capitol was in a lull.

The beatings continued, only now the boss had lost the respect of his staff.

Chapter 56

Flowers In The Dirt

I n late April of 1989, we finally got a listen to what Paul McCartney was up to. Ron Wiesner, who was Paul's U.S. manager, came to New York City to world premiere Paul's new album, "Flowers In The Dirt." We all huddled up at the world class Hit Factory recording studio with our guests. Ron played the music and showed everyone the beautiful cover art and video for the first single, "My Brave Face."

Ron Weisner came from Brooklyn and loved music growing up. He started his career in the mailroom and moved up to be the promotion assistant at MGM Records. We hit if off instantly. To have Paul's manager in my corner was the key to my success in promoting Paul to radio.

Everything was off to a great start. You could feel the energy surrounding Paul and his new work.

Eventually the single went top 5 at the adult contemporary format and top 25 on the pop charts.

We worked the album hard through the summer and I'd often hear from Ron about Paul's plans.

In the middle of August, he summoned me over to his hotel on Madison and 65th. The plush Plaza Athénée, a five-star luxury hotel. He told me Paul was going to do a press conference and small performance at the Lyceum and that it was all hush hush. He told me he wanted Scott Muni and the whole WNEW FM crew down there. Paul would be taking questions from the press, but Scott was to be backstage with a hot microphone to jump to the station live at any time.

Paul was getting ready for his first world tour in 13 years and to show off what was coming he and his band played for the press, radio and invited guests. Paul mentioned the tour would be coming to Los Angeles, Chicago, and conclude with four shows in New York City at Madison Square Garden.

It was an amazing launch. Yet as we continued to work the album, subsequent singles got less attention from the radio programmers. The album began to fall off the top 100.

Summer had come and gone.

Then the shit hit the fan!

Ron went ballistic! He sent a note to everyone at the company, from the top down, that he was extremely angry that Paul McCartney was about to embark on the U.S. leg of his world tour and his new album was at #161 and sinking in the trades.

He demanded to know what Capitol was going to do about it!

He was right! Yet we had already given radio three focus tracks from the album. There was no obvious fourth single capable of leading the charge back onto the chart.

Then a miracle happened.

Billboard said it loud and proud: "In the past four weeks 'Flowers In The Dirt' climbed 95 notches and is now at #98*."

Ron was pleased. He could show Paul how he kicked ass.

A few months later, the miracle was revealed. It was a hoax!

The *Los Angeles Times* ran a story that said:

"Suit Accuses Capitol Records of Trying to Falsify Data: An ex-employee says the firm ordered him to bribe retailers to help move its albums up *Billboard* magazine's sales chart!" It said record companies offer free concert tickets and additional advertising spending in exchange for retailers changing their sales figures.

When Paul's tour wound its way to New York City, Ron called me for a meeting at his hotel to go over the concert tickets. He wanted to make sure all the formats from radio were covered. Ron said Paul would do three radio interviews. One for the FM stations, which would be Scott Muni and his crew over at WNEW FM, one for the top 40 station, which was

Z100 at the time, and one for the adult contemporary radio station, WNSR.

He also told me Paul had four tickets in the front
row for all the concerts and wanted me to be responsible to get key people in those seats. It was a dream
come true.

On the day of the first show, I met up with Ron,
who took me straight to Paul's dressing room inside
Madison Square Garden.

Paul greeted me and asked me what I'd been up to
since we last saw each other. I told him I was now a proud
father and he beamed. He asked me if I had a photo
and I took one out to show him. He held it in his hand
and said, "I've got just the thing for this young lad!"

He jumped up and went over to his dressing
trunk. Inside a drawer was a U.K. version of his
recent single – something I hadn't seen before. It
had a big white blank spot on the front of it. He took
a pen and asked me my son's name. He autographed
it beautifully and then he began to draw a smiling
face on it. He said, "You won't get this little drawing,
BUT HE WILL!"

The following day, I was backstage early and
found myself again in Paul's room. We were waiting for WNEW FM to arrive. I started to ask him
about his early Hamburg days with the Beatles and
the massive repertoire of songs the Beatles com-
manded. I asked him about a song the Beatles sang
called "Clarabella" and he told me it was by a few of

the fellas in Bill Haley's group called the Jodimars. I thanked him and told him I asked John about it once and John said they nipped it off a B-side of a Little Richard single. I told Paul I spent years trying to find that Little Richard record!

The WNEW FM team showed up and, after handshakes, Paul continued to tell me about Hamburg. WNEW FM were checking the mics for the interview and were able to catch Paul tell me about recently being in Hamburg and seeing Astrid Kirshner, the woman who took the early pictures of the Beatles. Paul talked about the Beatles going to her home and how they appreciated the home-cooked meal Astrid's mom served.

The second show went terrific and a few of the WNEW FM folks went and sat in those front row seats.

By the day of the third show, Paul's manager Ron was looking exhausted but carrying on graciously.

Paul was going to finish up the radio interviews with the adult contemporary radio station in New York called WNSR. I got to the venue early and met up with the program director. We had always hit it off. He ended up marrying a gal from my hometown, so we were a great fit.

When I went to the production office to find Ron, they told me he had been rushed to the hospital with a possible heart attack.

It became chaos! Paul's publicist took over Paul's agenda and shut down all interviews.

I told the PD to wait while I looked into things. I went to Paul's room and we shook hands. The press guy was there and said Paul wasn't going to do anything except the soundcheck.

The hallway from Paul's room to the stage was packed. It was lined on both sides. I found the PD along the wall and told him the bad news. Before he could respond, Paul came out of the room and was heading to the stage. I watched him walk pass 50 people nodding but when he got to where I was standing, he stopped and put out his hand to shake! I was aglow! The PD gave me a glare I will never forget. He was pissed and about to blow his stack!

He told me over and over how he was promised an interview. How he waited outside a dressing room for an hour. He told me this would ruin him. I reminded him Paul's manager had a heart attack! He wouldn't back down. I told him I had front row tickets for him and his wife and after the show I would try everything I could to bring him backstage to meet Paul and perhaps make a time in the future for the interview. He got so angry he slapped my hand. The same hand Paul had shaken. He left in huff.

After I caught my breath, I realized I had two front row tickets for the evening's show – and no one to give them to. It was 7 p.m. and the show was going to start within the hour. I hit the exit and found myself on 33rd Street with tons of fans filled with excitement.

I didn't have to walk 25 feet before I ran smack dab into Keith and Eddie from Eighth Street! Keith and Eddie were my first Beatle friends. They wrote to me back in 1971 and we became lifelong pals. They had no idea what was about to go down. I asked them if they had tickets. Keith said they splurged for top dog seats, half way back and on the side.

Without making a big deal out of it, I told them I had two tickets Paul had given me that were terrific. I told them the tickets were up front and close but I didn't tell them it was the front row directly in front of Paul.

I got to watch them show their tickets and move closer and closer to the stage. I could see their bewilderment and excitement from 50 yards away.

Outside the Garden, there were a few fans without tickets. I walked up quietly to a couple and handed them Keith's tickets and quickly walked away. I looked back and could see the wonderful delight in their eyes.

It was Christmas time. It was New York City.

Paul McCartney was performing the Abbey Road medley on stage and I was in heaven.

Chapter 57

Bonnie Raitt

I met her on a Monday and my heart stood still! I was 20 years old and had a cool job of coordinating the record promotions between Warner Bros. Records and their distributorship, Warner, Elektra, Asylum Records. The biggest perk: all the free tickets that came my way.

That's how I came to see a young Bonnie Raitt play the very fabulous Max's Kansas City, a Park Avenue nightclub, one evening in April of '73. She was playing upstairs with Little Feat. Bonnie was covering deep blues artists like Mississippi Fred McDowell and Sippie Wallace. This was a learning curve for me. She was able to emotionally get into the soul of these long forgotten songs. She was so powerful I would have believed her if she said she wrote the lyrics and melody.

Warner Bros. Records was a haven for true artists. Folks whose work needed time to grow. Joe Smith, the president of Warner, wasn't giving up on Bonnie even though we couldn't crack the top of the sales charts. Years later, after Smith left the label, Warner Bros. dropped her for lack of sales.

In 1987, Joe Smith became the president of Capitol Records and, of course, he signed Bonnie.

In 1989, she made history. She delivered the "Nick Of Time" album and after 17 ½ years, Bonnie knocked it right out of the park!

Capitol Records took it to #1 in Billboard!

We sold FIVE MILLION COPIES!

She won three GRAMMY awards, including ALBUM OF THE YEAR!

Bonnie worked her tail off. She was a consummate professional. She went to all the radio stations to meet the staff and do interviews. Everyone fell in love with her.

Bonnie, being in recovery, was easy to work with. Gratitude, appreciation and her good will guided her.

"Nick Of Time" album played out at FM radio just like the Crowded House. The real connoisseurs of tasty music loved both records but in Bonnie's case, many programmers found the earthy tones and loose feel didn't fit the slicker sound that was being heard at the time. The top *Billboard* Album Rock Tracks included Def Leppard, Bon Jovi, U2, Bad Company and Guns N' Roses.

Finally, that big bass groove and fantastic interpretation of John Hiatt's "Thing Called Love" added up to a full blown smash hit. The FM stations locked on and the pendulum swung over to the sounds of Bonnie Raitt. Fortunately, "Nick Of Time" had multiple album tracks, including "Nick Of Time" and "Have A Heart," to keep the airwaves humming over the entire year.

Chapter 58

Just In The Nick Of Time

Capitol was on a high with Bonnie's "Nick Of Time." After all the toasts, all the sales, and all the airplay, the promotion staff got a note from the Vice President of Marketing. Everyone thought they were smelling a bonus when they opened the package.

He wrote the following.

"I want to personally thank each of you for the incredible job that you have done. This "Nick Of Time" project is a textbook example of a record company working directly and in tandem with CEMA, a great distribution company. Please accept this t-shirt as a gesture of our appreciation for your fine work."

A t-shirt? The VP of Marketing had the balls to send us a t-shirt after five million in sales and Album of the Year honors? Soon I realized it could have been worse. I spoke with someone over in the press department who said, "We got nothing!"

Just after morale plummeted to a new low, Capitol Records Distribution Center (also known as CEMA) appointed a new President. One of his first moves was to reach out to the promotion team. Finally, we were hearing from a sane voice!

His name was Russ Bach and he wrote:

"You have obviously noticed that this letter has been delivered to your home. That is because it's special and not just a memo you receive in the day to day communications cycle.

"This is my first attempt to address you. I wanted some special attention between us.

"To put the record straight, I was a promotion man between 1961 and 1966. I worked in the Chicago market when AM radio was all we had.

"I know full well the success and the failures of the promotion representative. I remember going from weeks of being shut out to the weeks of having pure ecstasy because I owned 25% of the top 40 chart. I always remembered the promotion rep is the backbone of the sales effort in the record business.

"You receive a piece of plastic with some sounds on it and you are expected to go out and get that product played. S0 here you are walking in with that 'intangible piece of plastic' in your hand that you don't really know will be a hit or not. You have got to go in and sell it like it was the 'hottest thing since sliced bread.' You have to go in and convince some programmer that by playing this record he will build his programming audience.

"The selling of an intangible is the hardest thing to do in the world of sales.

"I want to make the point to you of how important you are to the team and how important your input is at those weekly meetings. We need you there with clear, concise information regarding the product that you are working so that the sales reps can intelligently place that product in the field.

"We need your enthusiasm! We need your knowledge! We need you to boost all of our sales efforts in the field on a day in and day out basis."

As his introductory letter showed, Russ really knew how to connect with people and make them want to excel. His management style was wildly different from the one I'd grown accustomed to in nearly 10 years of weekly Capitol promotion calls.

Chapter 59

The Wild Man!

It was January of 1989 and time for another flog-ging of the promotion staff.

The phone rang. I picked it up. It was the smell of the rumpdog. He was ready to bite. The entire promotion staff was on the line too.

He began to rant.

"I'm in an airport and I don't want any dogs barking on the call! I'll tell you what. We had a ter-rible, terrible week. It's a letdown!! The competition kicked our ass!!!

"There were 16 records that got between 10 and 20 adds apiece and we had zero of them. We had none, zero, absolutely none! In the past, I've been able to say we haven't had product that's competitive, but that's not the case.

"Now let me tell you folks, it's countdown time to losing your jobs! When I see a situation where we're having trouble breaking 20 total adds as a team when we have real good records, that's fucked!

"When I sit here and I see 10-year promotion veterans going blank, zero, absolutely nothing on records, and I'm not talking about one or two. I'm talking about 7-10 people with a lot of experience in your markets with great records and zero adds!!

"I worked too damn hard to get to this point where we got quality product to let this dissipate in front of my eyes!!!"

The promotion call marked a new low. The boss was crushing the team he had built.

He continued.

"By god, I'm not gonna let it happen!! If it takes cleaning house, or me acting like a fucking jerk and being a wild man and losing my goddamn mind, I WILL!!!!!!

"Now I don't know what the hell happened out there this week, but I'll tell ya what, we got our butts kicked. It wasn't just the independents either. It was everybody that kicked our butts. We looked like hell and I'm not gonna have it, so here's what we're gonna do!!

"I want one add apiece on that board in my office!!! I don't care if it's Marc Almond's, 'Bitter Sweet,' I don't care if it's Tracie Spencer's cover of 'Imagine,' I don't care if it's Gina Go Go's, 'I Can't Face the Facts,' I don't care if it's a fill in add on Duran Duran's 'All She Wants Is,' or Wilson/Zander's, 'Surrender To Me'!!

"By Friday evening you will have an add on that board or I will have a WRITTEN EXPLANATION that is going in your personnel file as to why you, as a promotion manager for Capitol Records, were unable to go out into your market and secure one add for Capitol Records!!!

"I'm putting this into your file explaining why you don't have the wherewithal to go out there when the chips are on the line, when you are on the line, when you are called on to perform, that you cannot perform!!!!

"I want everyone on the road! Don't tell me you got dinner plans or some shit! Get on the road and get me some adds!!!!"

Well, that sure made people cry and feel crummy.

The Tracie Spencer version of the iconic John Lennon song, "Imagine," was amateur. It was a miss. Programmers gave it a thumbs down. She was 12 years old and had just won a contract with Capitol by winning a singing contest on television. No radio station in New York City was interested in starting her career. It flamed out at #85 in *Billboard*. That shows even the secondary radio stations didn't give a shit.

The Marc Almond single never charted and the album never made the *Billboard* top 100. What radio station would want to stick their necks out for Marc?

Gina Go Go had "Sweet Surrender," which didn't crack the top 75 in *Billboard*. Anyone in the world remember Gina Go Go?

Nobody could get these stiffs played. The boiler headed boss should have called in a few favors. He had no clout. His only shot to shake things up was to bury all of us. He lost everyone's respect and fucked up peoples' lives.

These records were bombs and would never be played in New York City or anywhere else and now the boss wants to write us up as not being able to get the job done. He was melting down in front of us.

Duran Duran had worn out their welcome at the top of the pop charts. They had split up into two camps, one called the Power Station and the other called Arcadia. Now they were back but the luxurious shine had faded. This new sound didn't fit what the fans wanted to hear. By this time, they limped along with just Simon, John and Nick, no longer the fab five. The single was "All She Wants Is," which no oldie station plays today. Nobody remembers it. It didn't even crack the top 20. They could no longer pull in some of the biggest markets that supported their previous efforts.

"All right, let's go over some records," the rump-dog yelled into the phone.

"We gotta hold off Paula Abdul's, 'Straight Up,' with our Sheriff single, 'When I'm With You.' Some stations are still not even top 10 on the Sheriff.

"We need to rescue Wilson/Zander!

"Duran Duran should be a top 20!

"Call a meeting with your salespeople and your customer service representatives and tell them you're at a critical point in the life of Capitol Records!!

"Ask them bluntly, 'Do you want to be a part of making a profit? Do you want to be part of the resurrection of Capitol Records? Do you want to help me with store reports?'

"Now GIVE AWAY THE WORLD! I DON'T CARE! For my records I want the world given away! I refuse to lose these two records. Give away all the Beatles' records you need to get the job done!!!!

"We MUST get 10 adds on Duran Duran this week!! Go sell your soul to the Devil!! I don't care!! We have to have 10 adds!!! You've got to promote the BIG Euro-house mix. I was talking to a lot of people this week that have not heard the mix or did not remember the Euro-house mix or were unaware that's the mix that's happening.

"We can offer phone calls from Gina Go Go and Tracie Spencer anytime!! Tracie got a goddamn standing ovation on Arsenio Hall for fuck's sake!!!!!

"Marc Almond is losing a hit record folks!! I don't care if we put the effort in and kicked ass. The record's not a hit and we knew it wasn't a hit and it never reacted and we didn't get phones and we didn't get sales and it didn't happen. We did everything possible for the record! Kiss its ass goodbye baby!!! BUT, when I know there's a hit record and we just let it dissipate away, slide off the fucking earth and go down in the goddamn pits where the bones of all the other goddamn hits that should have been, that's BULLSHIT! We got our own destiny and I'm tired of fuckin' worrying about it. I'm tired of losing sleep about it. I'm tired of getting fuckin' upset about it, so here's the deal.

"As men and women, as responsible adults, we have our own destiny in our hands! We have the ability, we have the capability, we have the tools to go out there and get the damn job done!! Now we either go out and do it or we don't!! My flapping my gums and my losing my voice and getting upset and standing here in a god damn Pan Am hallway sweating ain't gonna make a dip shit worth of difference. It's up to you to get out there and get your job done!! It's your responsibility as a mature adult and I want the damn job done!!!

"I'm going to be in London working the boys at Thorn/EMI so they understand what Capitol Records is doing so we don't have another fiasco! Last time they gave the David Bowie to EMI. I'm going over there with a purpose to impress these people with the work we have done and what we're gonna do and where we're at and if I'm there and the Duran Duran goes away and the Wilson/Zander record goes away and we lose Marc Almond and we don't get the Tracie and we don't get Gina Go Go all in the same week, you can best believe a change is gonna come.

"You better go down to fuckin' Tower Records and ask them for the RCA 'Sam Cooke Greatest Hits' and slap it on the fuckin' stereo and brothers and sisters 'cause, 'A Change is Gonna Come!'"

Boom! Dead silence. He hung up on us! He must have heard a dog bark!

Immediately my phone blew up with the local staff. They were either crying or blowing off steam. I never heard them so pissed off. After an hour or two, I needed a break.

It was time to tell this wild man to get over to Tower Records and buy a copy of Johnny Paycheck's "Greatest Hits" and play, "Take This Job and Shove It!"

Chapter 60

The Beatles & The Barber Of Seville

We had a huge regional meeting at the New York branch so that the staff could hear all the new music from all the labels. My presentation would follow the classical promotional guy.

I noticed in the new release booklet he was going to be presenting a new recording of the Rossini Overtures conducted by Herbert Von Karajan. He focused on a recording of the "The Barber Of Seville."

After he concluded, I pulled down the shades in the room and closed the door. I began to whisper.

"I've got something very special to play. It's an exclusive! We can't tell anyone what we are about to hear. Shhhhhhh!"

Everyone was looking around wondering what was going on.

Dave Morrell

"You've just heard the "The Barber Of Seville" and it was fantastic!

"Well folks, it's TRUE. YES, IT'S TRUE! Shhhhhhhhhh.......

"Capitol will be releasing THE BEATLES doing 'The Barber Of Seville!!'"

They thought this was bold and insane! Everyone was buzzing.

I took a cassette and loaded it into the machine.

To everyone surprise IT WAS THE BEATLES DOING "THE BARBER OF SEVILLE!"

Everyone was laughing as hard as they could!

Turns out the Beatles scatted the song over the ending credits of their movie "HELP!"

Even the classical guy was cracking up! Nobody had ever heard anything like this.

It was a terrific way to start a new release presentation. I had everyone's attention.

Little did I know at the moment, but the President of the company was in our presence!

I left the room to make way for the next presentation and headed over to a radio station so I missed the luncheon – and the chance to run into the President. But soon I would know exactly what he thought of my presentation.

Chapter 61

The Trifecta

A week later, I received a personal note from the President of CEMA.

It said:

"Dear David,

I just wanted to say thanks for the great product presentation you did on Friday morning. It was certainly very enjoyable hearing your presentation. I recognize that the N.Y. marketplace is not very easy for a promotion representative, however, with the attitude that you have, I don't see how you can fail."

Wow, that was the jolt of sunshine I needed on a cold March afternoon! It lifted my spirits to be recognized in such a personal manner.

A week later, while I was still on a pink cloud, the mailman arrived with a letter from the Wild Man to my home. I opened it with trepidation, considering the source.

"Dear Dave,

As we begin a new fiscal year, I would like to personally thank you for your efforts of the past twelve months. Our task has been to reactivate a label with a proud heritage. While the label has been performing at an acceptable level, it should have been expected to perform at a much higher level. 'Good enough ain't good enough.'

Turning a label around and accelerating it in the opposite direction is easier said than done. It takes a dedicated effort of the people who make up the label over an extended period of time to have visible effect. I have never witnessed a better job over a prolonged period of time than I have seen from my Capitol promotion team. Though times have been hard, we are about to reap the benefits of our work and become the hottest label on the street.

The cat who said success was 2% inspiration and 98% perspiration must have been thinking about us. Words cannot relate how proud I am of our efforts thanks to you."

I was pleased yet puzzled to get such a flattering note from the very rump dog that had threatened to clean house just a few weeks earlier. Had he turned over a new leaf? Found God? Or had Human Resources had a little chat with him?

To kick me up to a higher cloud, the V.P. of Rock Promotion sent me a note, which read:

"Dear Dave,

I want to let you know I think you are doing a terrific job. It's great working with you. Your goal over the next four months will be to 'educate and enthuse,' to an even greater degree, the Promotion Managers, District Managers, and Sales personnel in each of your districts.

We'll spread a positive attitude about rock artist development and product maximization.

Your excellent efforts and good spirit are really appreciated.

Keep up the great job!"

Chapter 62

Donny Osmond

I just couldn't get to sleep. My mind was running full speed. There was so much work to do and so little time. The new Joe Cocker single, "When the Night Comes," was sitting at 33 with a bullet on Billboard's Hot 100 singles chart and ready to be considered for Top 40 play in NYC. In the Big Apple the top stations only really played the top 15 over and over so it was going to be a combined effort from sales, press, and promotion. Everyone was expected to deliver. It was his first solo hit since 1975's "You Are So Beautiful."

On the album front, Paul McCartney's "Flowers in the Dirt" was revived since he was now touring America and it moved up from 129 to 98 with a bullet in Billboard.

I was also thinking of the upcoming Rolling Stones show in Atlantic City. It was the final show of their tour and artists like Axl Rose and Eric Clapton were going to join them for a pay-per-view event. My boss called me and told me to buy four of the most expensive seats from the promoter. He told me Tina Turner was going to need them.

Life was exciting and stressful, and resting was important, but I just didn't know how to do it.

I had to get up early to meet Donny Osmond and I needed rest.

It was 2:00 a.m.

The phone rang. I was pissed.

I picked it up and said hello.

It was Donny.

"What are you doing up?" I asked him.

"I just finished a show in Philadelphia and I'm heading your way. Can you please pick me up in the morning to take me to the radio station?"

"No problem," I said. I was thinking he was probably either at the Plaza, the Waldorf-Astoria or some other expensive hotel.

"I'm staying at the Red Roof Inn in the Meadowlands, in New Jersey!"

"Really?" I said in disbelief. I remembered driving by this joint and seeing a sign that said the rooms were 40 bucks a night.

Donny was a down to earth guy. I would also learn he's the hardest working man in show business. He worked for years to get his music taken seriously. One day, Jessica Ettinger, who was the music director of WPLJ, came upon an English import of a

Donny Osmond cassette and decided to put it on the air as a "mystery artist." The phones lit up, signaling a possible hit record, and Capitol signed him.

The song was called "Soldier of Love" and it reached #2 on the charts.

Donny worked it like a pro! Sometimes getting a record on the radio demands a strong-arm tactic, as he had found in Tampa, Florida.

The DJ's name was Cleveland Wheeler and he worked the top 40 Zoo down there. Donny said he was challenged to an arm-wrestling contest. If Donny won two out of three, Mr. Wheeler would add "Soldier of Love."

Donny got the add.

Not very scientific!

You think it takes charts and computers to figure out a hit record and then, boom, an opportunity opens up!

I finally fell asleep for three hours and rallied the next morning to get my ass in gear. It was December 1989 and very cold.

I drove over to the $40 a night motel in the Meadowlands and, to my surprise, standing outside in the cold waiting for me was the great Donny Osmond. His smile lights up the earth. A hearty handshake and off we went.

Over at the station, Donny had great fun and took some calls.

Donny was headlining the Palladium that night, performing his new album "Sacred Emotion," but immediately after leaving the radio station headed to an in-store over at Rockefeller Center. Like I said, he is the hardest working man in show business. Here was a guy who had played a gig in Philadelphia to a packed house the night before, was making calls at 2:00 a.m., getting up at 5:00 a.m., doing a morning radio station interview live in the studio and heading to NYC to do an afternoon in-store for two hours. All before soundcheck and performing his first show in 16 years, in front of a full house!

Another time we gathered in front of Radio City Music Hall to kick off the season with a live broadcast on WPLJ, the station that broke Donny.

Tons of people showed up and the area was blocked off. It was exciting and felt like Christmas. Everyone was in a good mood. As Donny was getting ready to go on the air he reached in his briefcase and then his pockets looking for a cassette of the song he wanted to play. He couldn't find it. He didn't panic at all, he's not like that.

He calmly asked me to go over to the hotel on 56th street, just a few blocks away, go in his room, grab the tape, and hurry back so he could have the radio station play it on the air. I hesitated. I told him how strange it would be to go into his room alone. He told me I had his permission and then he pushed the room key into my hand. He looked at me with pure trust. I hugged him and told him I'd be right back.

I raced over to the hotel, put the key in the door and voilà! I was in Donny's room. I saw the tape on the table and picked it up. As I turned to leave, I noticed one thing. His bed wasn't a mess after sleeping in it and near his pillow was a huge beautiful Bible, opened. It was profound. It was a beautiful, peaceful place to be if you're on the road working. It made me think about the way I leave a hotel room when I go out. It made me think about meditating and praying and finding peace to rest the soul. I wanted what Donny had. Serenity, love, compassion, tolerance and peace of mind.

Donny was a wise man who had learned to crush the ego.

One time at lunch he was talking about buying the family a boat. My eyes rolled thinking of how much a boat would cost! Then he said he just wanted a little Sears fishing boat that could hold eight. He figured it wouldn't even cost a grand. I sighed and smiled. I really loved Donny.

Once the hoopla of Donny having a big comeback hit had subsided, he invited the whole promotion staff to sail with him on his lawyer's yacht off Marina Del Rey. It was a big deal. Donny, who doesn't indulge, packed the boat with champagne.

From Donny's sober point of view, he wanted to thank us for all the hard work in helping him attain his goal. At one point, he asked us to join him at the back of the yacht for a toast.

As he began a formal thank you with glasses raised high, he began to get interrupted by a few loose lipped promotion men. After a few attempts to quiet down, Donny gave up and just yelled, "Enjoy!"

One of the guys from Capitol videotaped the cruise around Santa Monica Bay. In one scene, Donny takes a few lucky guys to the Captain's deck for a meet and greet. The Captain was cool, calm and collected when he was bombarded by the drunk promotion man, screaming questions like, "Hey, did you ever have threesome with a couple while out at sea?"

By the end of our voyage, I felt bad for all the behavior and endless drugs and drinking that Donny had to put up with. Yet he was always gracious and not the least bit judgmental.

In February of '90 Donny was a presenter on the 32nd GRAMMY Awards and he gave an award to the Traveling Wilburys. Donny knew I was a BIG Beatle fan, and since George Harrison created the group, he thought of me. After opening the envelope and reading the winner on national television, he put the GRAMMY card into his tuxedo pocket and sent it to my home.

God bless Donny Osmond!

Chapter 63

Hammer Time!

After my 10 year run at Capitol – and a short break – I wound up working for Al Coury, who had moved over to Geffen Records. In my early days at Capitol, Mr. Hollywood had told the promotion staff all about what it was like to work under Al. He recalled, "Al stepped on a lot of toes! He pushed aside the lame and the slow. He put sledgehammers on our desks to remind us to HAMMER HAMMER!"

Faced with dealing with a screamer, I had to think about the offer.

Geffen Records wanted me to be their New York guy and work records by Peter Gabriel, Cher, Oliva Newton-John, Aerosmith, Guns 'N Roses, Joni Mitchell, Robbie Robertson, Jimmy Page and tons more.

It was an offer I couldn't refuse and I got to work the old 45 once again!

It was my first job after Capitol, but it wasn't my last.

More than 25 years later, I found myself back at Capitol Records' iconic Hollywood Tower. I had relocated to the West Coast to take a position at an independent label.

It's November 15, 2016 and the occasion is Capitol's 75th anniversary party – a star-studded event with legacy artists like Bob Seger, Heart's Ann Wilson and MC Hammer, and the new guard, which includes Katy Perry, Beck, Halsey and Niall Horan.

It's a beautiful evening and the place is packed. In addition to current President Steve Barnett, I spot Joe Smith, Hale Milgram and Bhaskar Menon.

Out of the blue, I turn and someone says, "Hey Hammer, you remember Dave Morrell?"

"I sure do! Hey Dave, give me a hug!" MC Hammer says.

He continues, "Dave! Of course, you know they say it was Nat King Cole who built this beautiful Capitol Records Tower, right?

"Well, I'll give Nat a floor! I'll give Frank Sinatra a floor! I'll give the Beach Boys a floor! I'll give the Beatles TWO FLOORS!!!

"But me? FOUR FLOORS, DAVE!!!!!

"That's about right! I sold 40 million on my DEBUT ALBUM!!!!!!"

Hammer and I fell into each other's arms laughing. Before the night was over, Steve Barnett would present him with a plaque in recognition of 50 million albums sold worldwide over the course of his career.

As I recalled my time at the Beatles' U.S. label, the barking of the rump dogs was the last thing on my mind. I'd made a career of introducing people to some of the most wonderful, interesting music ever recorded. How could I be anything but grateful?

Chapter 64

When I'm 64

The following year, I hit a milestone. I turned 64. True to the Beatles song, I found myself doing the garden, digging the weeds. Sometimes, on Sunday mornings, we'd go for a ride. I was loving life in California. Santa Monica was far from the song's Isle of Wight, but idyllic nonetheless - except at rush hour.

Drawing from my years as a promotion man and a longtime Beatles collector, I had begun publishing a series of books, which brought me in touch with people from around the globe. Complete strangers wrote to me, finding a kinship in our shared love for the Beatles, and long lost friends reached out also.

The Beatle Butcher cover that John Lennon had given to me in 1971 had long since passed out of my hands. In the fall of 2017, I was startled to see a story about it going up for auction. It went for $100,000.

In 2019, it sold at auction in Liverpool for $234,000. I was flabbergasted. Julien's Auctions issued a statement saying it was a record price for a Beatles Butcher cover – and the third highest price for a vinyl record, behind Ringo's personal copy of the White Album, numbered No. 0000001, and Elvis Presley's first recording. The King had made it for his mother and there was only one copy.

A week later, I heard from the buyer of the Butcher cover. They wish to remain anonymous but I can say that the person is someone I've known for more than 20 years.

We got together and kicked back for a fun Beatle evening.

I asked why they would spend so much on an album cover with a big circle on it that says, "TO DAVE." For that kind of money, why not buy a "Sgt. Pepper's Lonely Hearts Club Band," signed by all four Beatles?

They replied that there were many "Sgt. Pepper" albums signed by the Beatles, but there is ONLY ONE OF JOHN'S BUTCHER COVER!

It brought me joy to know that, after having many owners, John's Butcher cover was now in the possession of a dear friend who loves the Beatles as much as I do.

It's been over 20 years since WNEW-FM, the pioneering New York City rock station I'd worked so closely with during my Capitol years, switched formats. The music that played them out was a fitting coda for the station – and for my own rock story also. It was "The End," the last song on the last album the Beatles recorded.

"And in the end, the love you take is equal to the love you make."

Made in the USA
Middletown, DE
26 May 2020

96089508R00168

vabfi

WILDE

VAL

DISCARDED

Valparaiso-Porter County
Library System

Wilde, Ameila, author
Ruthless kiss
33410015607106

01/07/22

RUTHLESS
Kiss